D1548040

Elizabeth's parliaments

QUEEN ELIZABETH IN PARLIAMENT

A. Ld Chancellor. B. Marquises, Earles &c C. Barons. D. Bishops. E. Iudges. F. Masters of Chancery G. Clerks. H. Speaker of ye Comons
I. Black Rod. K. Serieant at Armes. L. Members of the Commons house. M. Sr Francis Walsingham Secretary of State

Elizabeth's parliaments

Queen, Lords and Commons 1559–1601

T. E. HARTLEY

Manchester
University Press
MANCHESTER
AND NEW YORK

DISTRIBUTED EXCLUSIVELY
IN THE USA AND CANADA
BY ST. MARTIN'S PRESS

Copyright © T. E. Hartley 1992

Published by Manchester University Press
Oxford Road, Manchester MI3 9PL, UK
and Room 400, 175 Fifth Avenue, New York, NY I00I0, USA

Distributed exclusively in the USA and Canada
by St. Martin's Press Inc., 175 Fifth Avenue, New York, NY I00I0, USA

British Library Cataloguing-in-Publication Data
A catalogue record for this book is avaliable from the British Library

Library of Congress Cataloging-in-Publication Data
Hartley, T. E.
    Elizabeth's parliaments : queen, lords and commons, 1559–1601 /
T. E. Hartley
        p.   cm.
    Includes bibliographical references (p.   ) and index.
    ISBN 0-7190-3216-4 (hardback)
        1. Great Britain—Politics and government—1558-1603. 2 Great
Britain Parliament—History—16th century. 3. Elizabeth I, Queen
of England, 1533–1603. I. Title
DA356.H37   1992
942.05'5—dc20   91-37905

ISBN 0 7190 3216 4 *hardback*

Typeset in Scala with Clairvaux display
by Koinonia Ltd, Manchester

Printed in Great Britain
by Biddles Ltd, Guildford and King's Lynn

Contents

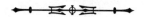

Preface

Students of Elizabethan parliamentary history have benefited recently from a number of studies which add to and modify the account of the House of Commons and parliamentary proceedings completed by Sir John Neale in the 1950s, though in many matters of 'story outline' that account remains essential reading. I have not set out to write a narrative account of Elizabeth's parliaments: for one thing that would have been impossible to do within the space available. Neither have I tried to provide a guide to matters already dealt with by historians who have focused on procedure and the 'business record', as Michael Graves terms it, or, indeed, to the process by which the House of Commons was elected. What follows is a reconsideration of the main areas covered by Neale's *Elizabeth I and her Parliaments* in the light of the attacks on it by the so-called revisionists. Important questions about the nature of government, the workings of Elizabeth's personal monarchy, and lawmaking suggest themselves, and I have chosen to devote this book to a consideration of them. The great divide between Neale and the so-called revisionists cannot perhaps be resolved, but it is possible to make sense of what happened in Parliament without the rigours of either approach, and without wholly sacrificing an overarching interpretative concept. Students of Elizabethan England are now beginning to benefit, however, from other perspectives. One of the more promising aspects of recent writing is the realisation that the clash between Neale and the 'revisionists' arose, in part at least, from approaches with differing priorities.[1] It is also clear that new approaches will increasingly draw historians' attention away from the central parliamentary arena into the towns and counties where the much of the demand for legislation originated. It will be evident that I have relied a good deal on Neale's outline of events – as indeed do his fiercer critics – though I do not follow his analysis. I have benefited in recent years from many conversations with Dr David Dean, whose work on the business of lawmaking and interest groups is a clear example of the newer lines of enquiry already referred to.

NOTE

1 Graves, *Elizabethan Parliaments*, pp. 75–80 is especially refreshing here.

Abbreviations

APC	J. W. Dasent *et al.* (eds.), *Acts of the Privy Council of England*
CJ	*Journals of the House of Commons*
Commons	P. W. Hasler (ed.), *The House of Commons, 1558–1603*
CRO	County Records Office
CSPD	*Calendar of State Papers, Domestic*
EP	J. E. Neale, *Elizabeth I and her Parliaments*
HMC	Historical Manuscripts Commission
LJ	*Journals of the House of Lords*
n.s.	new series
PE	G. R. Elton, *The Parliament of England*
Procs.	T. E. Hartley, *Proceedings in the Parliaments of Elizabeth I, i. 1559–81*
PRO SP	Public Record Office, State Papers
SR	A. Luders *et al.* (eds.), *Statutes of the Realm*

Chapter 1

Introduction

Research into aspects of Elizabethan parliamentary history in recent years has expanded our knowledge, not only in areas previously studied, but in new territory. So the student of Elizabeth's reign is offered fresh horizons as well as new perspectives. We are now beginning to build a picture, for instance, of the activities of groups of people who were attempting to secure legislation in Parliament: these groups may have represented boroughs, or craft or trade groups who were trying to advance particular causes.[1] The long-term benefit of this type of study will be enormous, if only because it will emphasise the point that Parliament could never really operate behind closed doors, simply because much of its work involved particular parts of the Queen's realm. Further research will also yield rewarding, if perhaps limited, insights into the activities of the House of Lords and the individuals who sat there. While the documentary evidence of debate in the Commons is far from abundant and unevenly distributed throughout the whole reign, the position for the House of Lords is much worse. No extensive reports of debates have come to light, so our view of what happened in the Upper House itself will always be limited. We can also expect that painstaking research will tell us more about procedure, and detailed work on the lives and careers of individual members will undoubtedly yield dividends.

Much of this lies in the future. The most recent approaches have developed from the major controversy about the significance of parliamentary proceedings. This is the central concern of this book. Sir John Neale's picture of conflicts between Elizabeth and the House of Commons had been generally accepted until well into the 1970s, but, as we shall see later, it has since been subjected to severe criticism.

1

Co-operation, not conflict, was generally the order of the day, it is now argued, because Parliament was an institution devoted to the business of making law, and not predominantly a *political* entity. The debate is not closed. The main focus in the following chapters will be on the areas germane to that central debate, and the conflicting views which form it will be reconsidered. It will be suggested that more attention should be devoted to the broadly held assumptions which informed the thought of the predominantly Protestant members of both Houses of Parliament. This is not to argue that all members of Lords and Commons thought in identical ways on all issues, but that there were certain basic starting-points common to most men, and further that these 'principles' can offer a way of understanding a range of parliamentary affairs. In this way, it is possible, for instance, to see why there was conflict in Parliament whilst not subscribing to Neale's view of it. At the same time it may become clear why some later commentators have been keen to stress that Parliament functioned – that is to say it got through a considerable body of lawmaking – because there was a good deal of co-operation between all the constituent parts, Crown, Lords and Commons.

It is tempting to compare Parliament today with that of the first Elizabeth. Now, it is the place of regular government. It is always in session for a set number of days a year, and the Crown, whose assent to legislation is still a constitutional requirement, is required to operate on a plane above the party politics of the day. Parliament's political functions and importance are clear, but it is an institution which has evolved. Its role and functions have changed to a greater or lesser degree over the centuries. The fact that the English Parliament has such a long history demands that we should be all the more wary of assuming that things were always as they are.

It cannot be stressed too much that Elizabeth I remained in strong control of government itself in a way which her present-day namesake cannot begin to emulate. There were thirteen parliamentary sessions in Elizabethan England, most of them lasting less than three months. Parliament was not an institutional fixture of life and government in the way it is now. Even so, during that time there were ten general elections, so these at least, in a reign of forty-four years, were as common an experience as they are today. The means by which county and borough members were returned to the Commons is beyond the focus of this book, and has been dealt with elsewhere.[2]

Elections in Elizabeth's reign did not, however, impinge upon the lives of as great a proportion of the population as they do today. In the sixteenth century the right to vote extended only to a minority of the adult population, to those in the counties who could, or who dared to, claim the forty-shilling franchise, and to those in the boroughs who could claim the right to vote under a variety of franchises. The active participation of everyone through voting was not considered essential. There was a belief that the Commons was nonetheless 'representative', for Sir Thomas Smith described it as the place where 'every Englishman is intended to be there present, either in person or by procuration and attorney of what pre-eminence, state, dignity or quality so ever he be, from the prince ... to the lowest person of England'.[3]

Whether the Commons were 'representative' or not, the idea that Parliament should determine the composition of the government and its policy was foreign to the age of Elizabeth I; the monarch and her advisers in the Privy Council and at court remained the centre of government. Parliament was called to 'give advice' for the safety of the Queen, the Church and the realm, as well as to grant money. It could not claim to be part of the policy-making government of the country. No one seems to have imagined that it should sit regularly, or more frequently, than it did. Peter Wentworth, who has often been seen as one of the great architects of the notion of Parliament's liberties and status, does not appear to have been concerned with the theoretical and constitutional ramifications of irregular sittings. Neither did he put forward the view that Commons, or Lords, ought to be supreme in policy or lawmaking – a supremacy which would have, in effect, depoliticised the Crown. Though there is reasonable doubt about the nature of Wentworth's concerns, words which positively dismantled the sovereign's role as policy-making governor-in-chief and the sole determiner of law (by royal assent) were definitely absent. Today, despite shortcomings which some argue bedevil our democratic process, we are still able to dismiss a government whose policies we do not like. In Elizabeth's reign the 'government', in the person of the Queen herself, was elected only by God, and, as she was fond of pointing out, answerable to God alone.

However broad or narrow the electorate may have been, it was not represented as the electorate is said to be represented in today's Parliament where parties have differing views, and elections reflect

3

levels of support for different policy platforms. It is hard to argue that in the sixteenth century issues of policy were major factors in elections. Parliament's infrequency prevented it from being an effective authority determining matters of national policy, such as war and peace and the conduct of alliances.[4]

NOTIONS OF POLITICAL CONFLICT AND CO-OPERATIVE BUSINESS

For about twenty years from the 1950s, the accepted picture of Elizabethan parliaments was one which bore some similarities to contemporary politics because it was based on a notion of 'an opposition' to 'a government'. Neale's view was that the Commons, especially in Elizabeth's reign, was keen to assert a political role for itself: at the beginning of the century Parliament had been 'essentially a legislative and taxing body'[5] For him, the reign was a landmark on the road to the Commons' 'future greatness'.[6] His account of proceedings was in practice a long essay on the development of the *Commons* at the expense of the *Lords*. His belief that there were attempts to expand the liberty of free speech in the Commons reinforced this notion of political development. Neale considered that Peter Wentworth was important here, because he wished to confront Elizabeth's determination to deny that the House had a right to discuss state matters. What Neale went on to show, however, was that the Queen remained steadfast in her opposition to the free discussion of religious matters, or, for example, those connected with her prerogative powers in financial matters.[7]

Neale believed that Elizabeth, though popular, faced an 'opposition', that is a group of men with a Protestant programme anxious to preserve England from the dangers of Catholicism.[8] Her plans for a religious settlement were changed by a group of radicals dominating the House of Commons, and she had to go further than she had originally intended (see Chapter 5). Neale also attached great importance to a small group of members whom he called the 'Puritan choir'. The existence of this group rested on a satirical document, the famous 'lewd pasquil', which described forty-three members of the Commons in 1566, sometimes with Latin tags or English verse.[9] He believed this to be a list of Puritan activists, the remaining members of the Commons being merely a 'parrot-like chorus'. It was the 'choir' which provided the dynamic for much of the conflict which characterised Neale's account of religion in the early sessions. Moreover, the campaign to produce further reform in the Church, including the Presbyterian programmes of the 1580s, offered further examples of organised Puritanism at work, and 'the House of Commons was militantly Protestant, ready nearly always to sympathise with its zealous and vociferous left wing of Puritans'.[10] However, with the defeat of Cope's Bill and Book in 1587, the cause suffered badly, and thereafter proceedings became less 'fanatical', in Neale's view (see Chapter 5).

Neale thought that the opposition was capable of planned attacks and campaigns in Parliament, usually the Commons, and that the 'choir' displayed a novel and strong 'genius' for organisation. His explanations of activity on Church matters in the House frequently relied on the notion that these members acted in concert with Puritan ministers outside Parliament. However, the 'Puritan choir' has no firm documentary basis. Scholarship has shown that the names mentioned in the verses were by no means all zealous Protestants. Indeed, only about half of them can safely be described as firm Protestants. The cornerstone of Neale's view has thus been undermined, with profound ramifications for the interpretation of the relationship between Elizabeth and her Commons which he saw as one of long-term conflict.[11]

Neither is it clear that a Puritan group planned action in Parliament in conjunction with clergy outside. The evidence Neale produced for such liaisons is speculative rather than clearly documented, and other scholars have argued that the actions of men in Parliament may have reflected the 'mood of the hour'. Nor is there much clear evidence that men like John Field influenced the decision of Job Throckmorton or other radical members to stand for Parliament in 1586. Neale argued thus, for example: 'There must have been party organisation behind him [Strickland], and if only we could penetrate to that background we should probably find the leaders of the radical clergy in consultation with a group of members of Parliament'.[12] It may not be necessary, therefore, to imagine that there was a sophisticated process of planning and co-ordination. Elizabeth's parliaments were occasions for the expression of such moods, and there were grave and urgent matters which naturally assumed enormous importance. Their occurrence did not depend on the activities of a minority. Overemphasis of the Puritan dynamic which formed the basis of Neale's account can distort our understanding of events. There were men in the Commons who must be recognised as radical Protestants – Strickland, Wentworth and Throckmorton, for instance – but to imagine that zealots like these were the sole embodiment of parliamentary concern for further reform of the Church is to misunderstand the breadth and depth of reformist thinking in Elizabethan England; and it fails to recognise that not everyone shared the same objectives.

The term 'Puritan' itself has been problematic to historians. It has often been used as far as Elizabeth's parliaments were concerned to indicate a divide between government and others, but historians are now inclined to see a larger range of religious unease, and to appreciate that some so-called Puritans might have been 'government men' as well as being Neale's 'rebels'.[13] More attention is now being paid to the notion of a 'broad consensus within the political nation' about the need for further reform. It is essential to establish clearly the nature of the proposals put before Elizabeth's parliaments and to determine the identities of their supporters. Within this framework there is even room to argue that the divide between the status quo and proposals for change hardened with the passage of time, so that men of moderation and standing may have been driven to more entrenched positions themselves. In other words, a dynamic of frustration affected events. Even so, proposals often had a broad, rather than a narrow appeal to Elizabeth's Protestant subjects who saw her Church and its bishops in need of control and further reform, and the more radical elements of Presbyterianism failed to gather general support in Parliament.[14]

But if a notion of an organised opposition with a programme has been seriously criticised, what of the context in which it was set? Neale's general picture was of a 'government' composed of Queen and Privy Councillors who defended a position of monarchic government against threatened encroachment from the Commons. The government relied not only on its own resources – in essence control of the nature and progress of parliamentary proceedings – but also on the authority of the House of Lords, a natural ally of the Crown, which did not sympathise with the rebellious Lower House.[15] Thus the Queen was never isolated for long on her own against them.

Recent criticism has modified this picture, in parallel with its rejection of the idea of a 'Puritan choir' and an urgent, constitutionally thrusting Commons. It has become more difficult to see the

Commons as willing to enter into conflict with the Queen in order to pursue its aims of self-aggrandisement. Parliament could not be the arena for an important constitutional contest since it lacked political importance and aims. Men were co-operative rather than confrontational, and where problems arose they reflected difficulties among Elizabeth's advisers as well as between the Queen and her subjects. They ran *through* the Lords and the Commons, rather than *between* the Commons and ministers, or between Commons and Lords. Therefore ministers, rather than a group of Puritans, may have tried to use the Commons to put pressure on the Queen. Moreover, Councillors needed to organise business in the House, and to drive it forward, and for this purpose they relied on a number of competent second-line members with whom they had direct links, like Thomas Norton and William Fleetwood. These were men with legal expertise, busy on committees and in debate, and prominent in drafting important measures. They were thus in the midst of 'government' business in the Commons; and it has been argued that they were employed even to the point of trying to rally parliamentary pressure against Elizabeth. Far from being in a body of opposition working against the government, therefore, Thomas Norton in particular, who had been seen by Neale as a prominent 'Puritan chorister', was actually *on the side* of Elizabeth's ministers.[16]

.Newer views have thus replaced one idea of a small group of activists in Parliament with another of a small group of Privy Councillors and 'men of business'. General observations about the way large institutions function suggest that a smaller part of the whole may have provided much of the dynamism. However, the notion that the Elizabethan Commons was driven in effect by a mere fraction of its total membership, while not inherently unlikely, needs to be treated carefully. So too does the judgement that it was a large, ineffective body, and that the Commons never had the political importance which some historians have supposed, since its members were not zealous in either participation or attendance. Firstly, our information about the 'speaking membership' is drawn mostly from journals or diaries which individual members compiled, for whatever reason, as their own account of the proceedings of the session. These accounts, unlike the official Hansard reports of today, are plainly not full records of all that was said. We are therefore at the mercy of the individual member who, unless he was skilled in the use of shorthand, would barely have been able to record all contributions fully, even if that had been his wish in the first place. It is likely that recording was undertaken on a far more selective basis, and was determined by what proved to be of particular interest to the individual member. It is also likely that star performances from Privy Councillors and the men of experience would be reported at the expense of contributions from lesser men.

It is instructive to compare two versions of the same debates where this is possible, for example, in the case of the Commons committee's debate on the subsidy in 1601. One young member, Hayward Townshend, provided a version of proceedings which is an apparently useful account of what was said, and recorded a number of contributions to the discussion. An independent account of the same meeting, however, shows that there were other members who joined in the argument. So the pool of speakers is greater than Townshend, an apparently first-class reporter, would lead us to suppose, and if this is true in this case then Hayward Townshend's report as a whole may under-record the number of members participating in debates. This leads on to an important secondary point. Debate in the Commons itself was not the start and finish of the business of the House. Increasingly, the afternoons were taken up with committee work as more measures were subjected to commitment as part of their progress through the House. For most of this committee work there is no record and we therefore miss important information which might easily, if the 1601 subsidy committee is anything to go by, throw much light on the activity of a larger number of members.[17]

A second connected point concerns attendance in the Houses. It appears that a large proportion of the total membership of both Houses was absent from proceedings on many days, and this evidence has been used to support arguments stressing Parliament's lack of real political importance.[18] However, since the introduction of the television cameras in 1989 it has become clear that many issues aired in the House of Commons – often of central importance to the government of the country – attract the presence, and possibly the interest, of only a small number of MPs. The level of attendance is in a state of near-constant flux: members simply do not take their seats at the start of the day and remain there for the duration. It may be regretted that then, as now, members were not more attentive, but we need to accept that even in the case of Thomas Cromwell and Hayward Townshend, two keen observers of the Elizabethan parliamentary scene, there were days when they were simply unable, because of other commitments, to attend the Commons and record what was happening.[19] It has yet to be established that the Elizabethan Commons were *especially* guilty of absenteeism, and in any case it is hard to use levels of attendance as a direct and precise barometer of political importance.

It looks as though Elizabethan members were a mixed bag of characters, as members are today. The picture of a body of men whose talents and contributions to the work of the Commons varied considerably in degree and kind is hardly surprising: plainly, it seems that some members were considerably more active than others in their participation. But the notion that the Elizabethan Commons was driven in effect by a mere fraction of its total membership should be treated carefully. The journals which record debate in the House show a relatively small number of the members as active speakers, apart from those who were Privy Councillors and a few others. There were without doubt the 'professional' parliamentarians, including Norton and Fleetwood, who were responsible for much hard work involved in the routine business of the Commons. They were prominent speakers, committee members and draftsmen and were thus invaluable 'servants' of the House, because they had a legal background which qualified them to play such a major part in what was a gathering of lawmakers. Yet their intensive activity does not necessarily imply that other members never took an active part in proceedings. The record is not complete.[20]

Both Privy Councillors and the so-called men of business could be long serving, but there were others not in these categories. Robert Wroth was perhaps the longest-serving member of all, starting his career in 1563 and continuing in every session thereafter. But there were plenty of others with less striking, but respectable, records. Members of the Hastings family in Leicestershire represented their county in six parliaments, and it was not uncommon for families elsewhere to provide members for their counties for three, four, or five parliaments, thus providing an element of stability in representation. There were men, however, who were not residents of the constituencies they represented, and among the borough seats this was especially so. Francis Alford served for Newton (Lancashire), Mitchell (Cornwall), Reading, Lewes and East Grinstead, apparently using the patronage of Lord Buckhurst and others at court to secure his seats. He seems to have had hopes that his parliamentary career would qualify him for greater things. Unfortunately, his marriage to a practising Catholic and his insistence on pursuing a scrupulously 'fair' line as far as Mary Stuart was concerned, while the bulk of the Commons was clearly intent on her death, meant that he was often out of tune with his parliamentary colleagues, and perhaps almost seen as a reactionary oddity. A trip to France also may have exposed him to the suspicion that he consorted with Stuart partisans: he was not able to establish sufficient credit with the Queen herself to ensure further progress. However, his participation in debate and committee work was extensive enough, and in this respect he could be considered to be a fully participating member of Elizabeth's Commons.[21]

Alford serves to remind us that Parliament was not wholly Protestant in Elizabeth's reign. The 1563 act for assurance of the Queen's power required members henceforth to take the oath of supremacy, so ostensibly there were no avowed Catholics in the 1571 Parliament or after. Biographical studies of members of the Commons show, however, that a substantial minority of members were either Catholics themselves, or counted Catholics among their close families. This is important, as we shall see, because it must be set against the strong Protestant line which was often evident in proceedings. The latter provided an important part of the framework for understanding Parliament's business with which we are here concerned. The presence of members whose commitment was less than Protestant, however, is one of several reasons why it would be wrong to suppose that the Houses were in the grip of a blind Protestant fanaticism.

Some of the members who spoke in the Commons were clearly impressive. Both Norton and Yelverton were described as eloquent. But inevitably in the large group of men which assembled in the House, there were others who were more tedious and those who, when they spoke, left their audience far behind. While Fleetwood himself was described by one commentator at the time as speaking 'learnedly and withal pleasantly', others did not find him so engaging and his contribution on one occasion was thought to be long, tedious and irrelevant. Again, in 1601 Hayward Townshend reported that he was not able to follow the argument of Mr Phettiplace one day because he used 'merchants' language'.[22]

There were many other members who seem to have been wholly or largely silent: perhaps they were the majority. Some of these may well have done very little, and possibly they did not attend much at all. Others, however, were likely to have made positive contributions. Men like Thomas Browne and Henry Cocke are good examples of members who assumed a role in local government and administration, and came up to Westminster on more than one occasion. As far as we can tell, Cocke contributed to only one debate, but they were both appointed to numerous committees, Browne to those concerned with Catholic priests, weights and measures and preservation of woods, for example, and Cocke to those dealing with fraudulent conveyances and linseed sowing, among other things. We cannot say with any confidence that they attended these meetings, or if they did, whether they spoke; but equally we cannot assume that their role was wholly negative, that they were willing in other words to allow the Nortons and Wroths and Cecils of the parliamentary world to rule the roost completely. For all we know they, and many more like them, played an active and positive part in the committee work of the Commons which made an increasingly positive contribution – albeit unspectacular and unrecorded – to the lawmaking activity of the House.[23]

THE IMPORTANCE AND ROLE OF PARLIAMENT

This book does not set out primarily to demonstrate the validity or otherwise of 'older' interpretations, or indeed of the 'newer' ones which view Parliament, and the Commons in particular, as an occasional cockpit for factional disputes, or for the subtler – or cruder – manifestations of disagreements among Privy Councillors and Queen. The networks of relationships between members of the Lords, Council and Commons may from time to time have been deployed politically in Parliament, but historians have yet to demonstrate this conclusively. Our concern here is with Parliament as a place where potentially influential men openly disagreed with the Queen, and where disagreement went beyond a small dominant clique of radically religious, or even a disgruntled, perhaps divided, band of the Queen's close advisers. Political criticism of the Queen permeated the Commons, and even the Lords. Few historians have argued that opposition was wholly absent from Parliament, or that the Queen could believe that members of the Commons in particular were harmless and well-disciplined men, intent on nothing other than making law as part of their partnership with the Lords and the Crown itself. However, the abandonment of the idea of an organised opposition as such has led to a belief that Parliament was therefore stripped of the political power, or nuisance value, which Neale gave it. He never argued in fact that the Commons were able to drive home their bold claims to a succesful conclusion, for at the heart of his belief in an increasingly important Lower House there was a steadfast belief that Elizabeth's political genius carried her through all the challenges. Her tactics were always well judged and supreme, and even when she was apparently compelled to adjust her reactions to events he considered this a demonstration of her ability to stoop to conquer. But the removal of one organised opposition from the scene and its replacement with another, albeit one supposedly organised, or orchestrated, by the Queen's own Privy Councillors, demands further and fuller reflection.[24]

By exploring the agendas which were given to Parliament and enunciated at the beginnings of the sessions by the Lord Chancellor or Lord Keeper we will be able better to understand Parliament's *raison d'être*. The tasks of making law and granting taxation – two enduring and nearly constant features of Elizabeth's parliaments – offer some indication of the rationale of parliamentary activity. The simple point that money was granted and laws were made for certain major purposes allows us to establish a framework of reference which gives a clue to the overriding concerns of many of the participants on the scene. Political assumptions and expectations are revealed, and we can begin to understand members' overriding concerns: the safety of the realm from the attacks of its enemies, the durability of the Crown and the succession, and the state of the Protestant Church. Given these concerns, and given Elizabeth's firmly held line over many issues, we need to ask how readily the regime, or the polity, was able to deal with the tensions which seem to have arisen. Moreover, the Lords, a smaller body of men closer to the Queen by virtue of their positions as courtiers, councillors, aristocrats and bishops, must also have been concerned about these matters. It is important therefore to explore the ways in which the Lords may have demonstrated an affinity with the Commons in spite of the Queen's wishes. Historians have recently complained about a long-term neglect of the House of Lords, and the balance has been re-dressed to an extent.[25] Though there may be reasons why we may never have as deep an understanding of events in the Upper House as we do of proceedings in the Commons, there is no longer any need to ignore the peers completely. While the make-up of the Lords was in obvious respects quite unlike that of the Commons, in other respects there were important affinities between the two. In Elizabeth's reign these were, at times at least, more important than any divide (see Chapter 6.)

Parliament was the place where the basic stuff of what Elizabethan England was about came under scrutiny; and because of this it is important to look at Peter Wentworth's contribution again, if only because his words, which seemed to Neale to be so important in Parliament's onward march to its constitutional pinnacle, continue to disturb us 400 years on. Whether he was ahead of his time in articulating a yearning for extensive parliamentary liberties, or more accurately, out of tune with most of his colleagues on the parliamentary scene *because* he was too visionary, needs closer scrutiny. Whatever the case, his single most dramatic utterance – that even Elizabeth was not faultless – remains a poignant voice of urgent complaint about the handling of a major policy issue by the sovereign prince of the realm.

In a sense, the one concern which permeated Parliament was simple. At the heart of much of Parliament's contemplation was the role of the Queen as sovereign of the realm. Historians have rightly commented extensively on the 'glory' that was a part of Elizabeth's reign, and more particularly on the elaborate celebration of the Queen's personality.[26] Yet one point is abundantly clear: the Queen's position, dignity and prerogative – all of which were reinforced by the Elizabethan personality cult – must be considered alongside her subjects' expectations of her. The famous 'golden speech' of 1601, in which the Queen explained her action over the vexed question of monopolies, in a way provides her own view of what her subjects had properly expected of her throughout her reign, as well as her unsurprising claim that she had fulfilled them. The crisis over monopolies itself provided another illuminating insight into the relationship between prince and subject which had been worked out over more than forty years: it was a major episode in the proceedings in the last session of the reign, and is examined closely in a separate chapter here.

Elizabeth's parliaments

It is easy to see how by today's standards Parliament in Elizabethan times may be seen as having little real political significance. But as the only means of providing a real basis for the legal implementation of policies it was unsurpassed in its pre-eminence, and Elizabeth used it for her own purposes as a major prop against attempts by others to encroach upon her sphere of active policy-making in Church affairs. While members of the Commons and Lords did not see themselves as necessarily subsuming 'the government' in the way that members do today, some of their numbers were in Elizabeth's government. Moreover, members were 'governors', because they were usually drawn from the ranks of the Justices of the Peace and magistrates who were charged with the implementation of laws which they themselves had often been instrumental in passing. Elizabeth also developed the notion, most clearly set out in Bacon's famous speech in 1571, that Parliament's principal role was its concern with legislation for the commonwealth, thereby keeping it off her own terrain. Although she retained the supreme political power of deciding which measures might go forward to the statute books, as far as commonwealth legislation was concerned, Elizabeth acknowledged a separate sphere in which Parliament could operate without the kind of jealously watchful eye she apparently kept on other proceedings.

Parliament's importance may be related to the idea that it was in some way representative. The subject is of great interest if only because in many ways Parliament at this time can hardly have seemed less so. We have already seen that today's concept carries with it the notion that all adults may choose members if they care to exercise their voting rights, that broad political programmes are voted for and against, and that Parliament itself is a political entity in a way that its sixteenth-century predecessor was not. Intervals of three or four years between parliamentary sessions, therefore, did not bring governmental paralysis in the sixteenth century, though shortage of money, for example for war, could easily lead to the reassembly of Parliament for financial assistance. Certainly such intervals between parliaments did not appear to be constitutionally alarming. The Commons perhaps resembled a gentlemen's club, rather than a gathering of men bound by a notion of representing the interests of several million Englishmen and women. We know that the franchise was limited, and there was no procedure whereby the members of the

Commons were required to act in consultation with their constituents who had, in any case, handed over 'full and sufficient' power to them to act. Neither consent or accountability were present in the parliaments of Elizabeth then, and no one apparently thought that every member of the adult population should be represented by virtue of being included in one of the parliamentary constituencies sending members to the Commons, though Smith, as we have seen, said that the whole realm was taken to be present there.[27]

Despite the absence of direct responsibility through an extended franchise, there was nevertheless a notion that members of Elizabeth's Commons spoke for others, as well as themselves, and that 'others' included all sections of the population. This notion was different from today's concept of representative assemblies, but contemporaries felt it to be significant and used it to explain the importance of the House. When Strickland was detained and prevented from attending the House for several days because he had introduced without authorisation a bill which would have changed the Elizabethan Prayer Book, members complained that his constituents were being denied his service. A concept of public duty was thus invoked to give force to a protest against the Queen's attempt to discipline a member: he was not in the House as a 'private man, but to supply the room, person and place of a multitude, especially chosen and therefore sent'. There may even be in these words a hint of a link between Strickland and his constituents which recent commentators do not generally recognise, preferring to see the member–constituent relationship as impersonal rather than personal. It seems though that as the reign progressed the personal link became clearer as at least some constituents paid heed to the quality of their prospective members and a number of general 'issues' emerged at election times, in particular a strong preference for those with a solid commitment to Protestantism. A remarkable testimony to this appeared in a letter written to Burghley by Robert Beale, clerk to the Council and enthusiastic worker for Church reform, in which he lamented the lack of progress for his cause. In frustration he explained how Elizabeth had been requested on many occasions to take the matter in hand by the Commons which represent, he said, 'many millions of her Majesty's subjects'. It is not clear whether Beale is arguing that religion ought to be taken up because the Commons said it should be. However, he does say in clear tones that the Commons' role in this matter derives from the fact that they represent so many people.[28]

The following chapters explore many of these themes more fully, some of which cover ground which has been worked and re-worked by many hands in attempts to provide new insights. Whatever modifications have been made recently to Neale's interpretation of events, it remains the case that the narrative framework set out in his two volumes remains largely unassailed; so it has not been thought necessary to repeat it here except in so far as it is essential to the argument. So a comprehensive survey of parliamentary proceedings is not offered, and neither can it be claimed that all problems have been resolved. The nature of historical inquiry, certainly on the scale which is now developing with respect to Elizabethan parliamentary history, dictates that problems be constantly reviewed and redefined, and that new ones be identified. The intention in this book is to indicate the way the current state of thinking has evolved, and where new lines of inquiry may lead in the future. Principally, however, by considering how Elizabethan parliaments functioned and were told to function it will become clear that their importance was far from negliglible, though the yardstick of political, or even constitutional, achievement applied by some commentators is an inappropriate one. What was attempted, what was said, and who said it, may be far more significant because they are guides to the state of the political nation and the nature of political cohesion at the time.

NOTES TO CHAPTER I

1 See especially Jones and Dean (eds.), *Interest Groups and Legislation in the Elizabethan Parliaments*.

2 See especially Neale, *Elizabethan House of Commons*; Kishlansky, *Parliamentary Selection*.

3 Elton, *Tudor Constitution*, p. 241.

4 See below, p. 14, this chapter.

5 *EP*, i.16.

6 *EP*, i.21.

7 *EP*, ii.438–9.

8 *EP*, i.28.

9 *EP*, i.91–2.

10 *EP*, i.28.

11 *PE*, pp. 351–4; for a historiographical summary see Graves, *Elizabethan Parliaments*, pp. 18–21.

12 *EP*, i.195; Collinson, *Elizabethan Puritan Movement*, pp. 162, 278, 306, 398.

13 Graves, 'Thomas Norton'.

14 Lake, *Anglicans and Puritans?*, p. 7; Collinson, 'Puritans, men of business', pp. 189, 197, 204.

15 *EP*, i.40–1.

16 Graves, 'Management', pp. 17–21; *PE*, e.g. pp. 355–74.

17 Hatfield MS 89, fos. 82–3; BL Stowe MS 362, fos. 85–8v.

18 Graves, *Elizabethan Parliaments*, pp. 31–4; Haigh, *Elizabeth I*, pp. 107–8.

19 E.g. BL Stowe MS 362, fo. 250.

20 Graves, 'Management', pp. 17–21.

21 *Commons, passim.*

22 *Procs.*, pp. 181–2, 209, 213, 223, 312; Oxford, Bodley Rawlinson MS A.100, fo. 60.

23 *Commons, sub* Browne, Thomas and Cocke, Henry.

24 See Chapter 6; Graves, 'Management', p. 14.

25 E.g. Graves, *Elizabethan Parliaments*, pp. 18, 20, 29–31;*PE*, p. 17.

26 See especially Haigh, *Elizabeth I*.

27 See above, p. 3; Dean and Jones, 'Introduction', pp. 2–4; Neale, *Elizabethan House of Commons*, p. 158.

28 *Procs.*, p. 238; Collinson, 'Puritans, men of business', pp. 201, 205; Dean and Jones, 'Introduction', p. 4, Hartley, 'Sheriff and county elections', pp. 186–7; Hirst, review of Kishlansky, pp. 429–30.

Chapter 2

Lawmaking

Recent accounts of Elizabethan parliaments stress the importance of their 'prime function', that is, their legislative activity. The amount of time spent on matters of major state importance was limited, and Elizabeth did not generally allow legislative inroads into her own domain, particularly the religious one. The Lords and Commons were drawn from a small political and governing elite, and they used Parliament to pursue their own interests, personal, local, trade and so on. Because they needed the Queen's assent to any measures thus agreed among them, a co-operative spirit, rather than conflict, was necessary. It would be unreasonable to expect *perfect* harmony, but despite the occasional differences of opinion on big issues, there was general agreement.[1]

The Queen herself clearly needed new laws from time to time, and she did not hesitate to emphasise Parliament's importance in under-pinning the new regime. The acts of supremacy and uniformity in 1559 provide clear examples. After Parliament had confirmed her resumption of the supremacy she said through the mouth of the Lord Keeper that 'no manner of determination in Parliament neither can nor ought by any private man to be infringed or undone'.[2] In 1572 Robert Bell, an eminent lawyer and the Speaker-Elect, attempted to demonstrate the need for strong parliamentary statute to deal with the threat posed by Mary Stuart. He cited historical examples of 'ordinances and constitutions' which, because they lacked parliamen-tary confirmation, were 'perilous as well in not sufficiently providing for those which deserved well, nor sufficient authority for punish-ment of them which deserved contrarie'. As far as Bell was concerned it was because of its efficacy in providing answers to important problems that Parliament was summoned so soon after the previous session in 1571. Elizabeth herself dashed the hopes of Bell and others on this occasion, but there were times when other measures were successful: in 1581 the Chancellor of the Exchequer, Sir Walter Mildmay, spoke of the need to provide against evil Catholic subjects at home as well as the enemy abroad, and the act against Catholics duly emerged.[3]

MAKING AND REVIEWING LAW

It is true that important matters like these occupied only a small proportion of Parliament's work. However, when we speak of Parliament as a legislative body we should define its task as one of legislative *review*. This often meant the rejection of bills, or existing acts, as well as the acceptance of newly proposed laws. It could also involve the confirmation, or rejection, of current statutes which had come up for review at the end of the life-span which Parliament had originally given them. We can perhaps most readily appreciate this task of legislative review by examining some of the formal activity which took place at the start of a new parliament. Close examination of the opening speeches of the Lords Chancellor, or commonly the Lords Keeper Elizabeth appointed in their stead, yields important guidance about what we may call the working principles of law review.

When Lord Keeper Bacon addressed the Houses in 1559 he spoke of the need for Parliament to 'reform and remove all enormities and mischiefs which could be harmful to the civil orders or policies of the realm'. They were to discover:

> what things by private wealth's devise have been practised ... contrary or hurtful to the commonwealth of the same for which no laws be yet provided; and whether the laws before this time made be sufficient to redress the enormities they were meant to remove; and whether any laws made but for a time be meet to be continued but for a time or presently to cease; besides, whether any laws be too severe and too sharp, or too soft and too gentle. To be short, you are to consider all other imperfections of laws made and all the wants of laws to be made, and thereupon to provide their meetest remedies respecting the nature and quality of the disorder and offence, the inclination and disposition of the people, and the manner of the time.[4]

Much the same message appeared when he spoke in 1563, though the report of his speech indicates that he stressed that laws which were too soft could endanger an innocent person, and laws which were too harsh 'may put in peril both the nocent and innocent'. Too many laws could breed 'so many doubts that the subject is sometime to seek how to observe them, and the counsellor how to give advise concerning them'. These elements appeared again in 1571,[5] and again in 1597 when Lord Keeper Egerton told the houses to prune laws where they found 'superfluity' and to supply any defects. In 1593 and 1601 efforts were made at the start of the sessions to ward off attempts to make new law since Elizabeth, perhaps more urgently than ever, seems to have wanted sessions uncluttered by business other than the speedy granting of subsidies. However, in 1601 the Speaker himself reasserted the parliamentary legislative role when he claimed that the session had been called to consult of laws 'being a thing impossible that the same laws should be fitting for all times'.[6]

There are many elements here, then: the need to make new laws, and also to consider repeal or amendment where current legislation was inadequate, superfluous, or oppressive. The Houses were also to ensure that laws were comprehensible so that lawyers might be able to give sound advice to clients. Lords Chancellor and Keeper were anxious to see that law was enforceable and accessible. Accounts of proceedings in two bills in the 1576 session illustrate these points, namely the Bills of Apparel and Forests. They are often cited as examples of tension between Lords and Commons, but their true significance is that they clearly reveal the practical, critical common-sense approach members could bring to their legislative work, albeit perhaps within a framework of some self-interest. The Bill for Apparel took its place in a long series of so-called sumptuary legislation which sought to regulate the subjects' garb. This government measure was introduced in the Lords, and was designed to strengthen an earlier statute of 1533 by stiffening its penalties against those dressing beyond their station. However, it failed to become law because the two Houses could not agree on changes before the session ended. The Commons objected in particular to an apparent enlarging of the royal prerogative entailed by the bill. It would allow the Queen to specify by proclamation what it was legitimate for the various degrees of men and women to wear. Criticisms also arose from considerations of reasonableness and equity. Thus, the punishments proposed did not fit the crimes envisaged; arrangements for making the

Queen's proclamation known to all subjects were inadequate, and could therefore lead to the prosecution of people who were innocent of their offence; and the notion of instant penalisation – by officers whom the Commons clearly thought could be of status insufficient to warrant their exercise of authority over men of their own standing – was rejected in favour of due process by trial.[7]

The second measure, the Forests Bill, was also designed to reinforce an earlier act. Disagreement between Lords and Commons again appears to have smothered it.The Commons took a stand on what they regarded as an unnecessary bill, because they said that a Henrician law, which tried to enforce the King's rights in his forests, already provided for the efficient administration of justice in the forest courts. They said the bill was also unreasonable because it required people to appear in whichever of these courts the judge decided, rather than the one in their own county, which was generally the current practice. There was thus a danger that the bill could involve increased and unnecessary expenditure of time and money in travelling to distant court hearings. Another concern, which may again signify an unease about yielding excessive powers in an act of Parliament, related to the kind of justice to be administered in the forest courts under this proposed new law. The bill said that process should be according to the law and 'to the customs, usages, and ordinances of the forests'. This the Commons said was:

> doubtful and uncertain, the same being known only to the officers
> and ministers of the forests and are so far from the common knowl-
> edge of other men as few or none that are learned in the laws of the
> realm have any understanding in them, so as if any subject of the land
> should be impeached for an offence ... he shall not be able to receive
> advice by counsel in the law for his reasonable defence.

It was also observed that

> in making of laws one principal and special care is to be taken, that
> nothing pass in dark words, but that all may be clear and evident to the
> understanding of the makers, thereby to know to what they bind
> themselves and their posterity.[8]

The concern about vesting too much power in the hands of petty officials which emerged in the Apparel Bill surfaced in other areas too. It was reflected by Mr Sampole, one of the lawyer–members of the Commons in 1571, when he argued that tax-collectors, being 'but mean men appointed to that office', often converted the taxes to their own use: he 'therefore wished the better sort of every county should be assigned to that charge'. Whether he was arguing that the gentlemen who became Justices of the Peace should also become collectors is not clear: normally they were responsible for *appointing* them; but Sampole's aversion to the 'meaner sort' is not in doubt. In the realm of finance in particular, men in Parliament often displayed a reserve about the Crown's powers, a concern revealed very obviously in connection with the royal rights of purveyance. An act of 1555 had given the Justices regulatory powers over the royally-appointed local purveyors, those men commissioned by the Crown to buy provisions for the Household at discounted rates. This act was clearly not successful, and further parliamentary attempts to deal with the problem in Elizabeth's reign proposed strengthening the Justices' authority.[9] It is not hard to detect attempts by the governing gentlemen to preserve their (local) interests in all this. An act to control the activities of the Queen's revenue officers in the localities has been descibed as 'inadequate'. Though they were sometimes corrupt, and the subject, as well as the Queen, could suffer in consequence, controlling them was not easy. The revenues they handled made them men of power and influence, for they could be used to finance land transactions. Government hopes of improving local administration by preventing sheriffs showing favour to influential men in their counties were not successful either. It was apparently hard to secure an impartial performance of duty.[10]

As the regime lacked a nation-wide bureaucracy this sort of institutional weakness may have been inevitable, but it did mean that the scope of what central policy-makers might attempt was limited. So the bill to control the export of grain in 1571, though apparently official in origin, was heavily revised in the Lords. Despite Burghley's presence, it left the localities with the crucial power to investigate current price levels at which export of grain was to be allowed, though this was a power admittedly exercised under licence from the Council. It may be that this was a sensible provision in view of the sensitivity of price movements to local conditions and the need to act quickly in order to take advantage of prevailing market conditions, but it does seem to mark a retreat from what had been the original intention of the bill.[11] There was also an evident concern in Parliament about what has been called 'delegated powers of legislation'. In 1576 Burghley, who had for some time been trying to secure the full payment of customs duties by restricting the landing of imported goods to daylight hours, proposed to designate a number of ports of entry for imports. The Commons suspended this measure, and the Lords suspended its successor in 1581, apparently disliking the fact that royal commissioners appointed under the act would decide which ports were to be so designated. In these cases there seems to be a wariness about leaving laws uncertain and allowing extensive powers of discretion to others in such an important area. Specific designation in the body of the bills may have been more agreeable.[12]

LEGISLATIVE INITIATIVES

The labour involved in dealing with all the bills which came before Lords and Commons was considerable. There was a largely standard process by which bills were read, and could progress through the two Houses to await the royal assent, in this reign. The three-reading procedure was essentially the norm, being repeated in essence in both houses.[13] However, it is difficult to compute precisely the number of bills coming before the two Houses and being subjected to at least part of this whole process. It appears that more than 1,360 bills were considered – though the figure may have been closer to 1,500 – and that more than 400 became acts. There could thus have been less than a one-in-three chance of a measure progressing through to the statute books, though a greater proportion of the major measures which dealt with the safety of the realm in one way or another probably stood a better chance, while other 'minor' bills enjoyed little real prospect of success.[14]

This naturally raises the problem of who was responsible for the introduction of these bills. In many cases there cannot be much doubt about where the initiative lay. For example, the supremacy, uniformity and Queen's title bills of 1559 were introduced into the Commons probably under Secretary William Cecil's official sponsorship, as was another measure for the consecration of bishops. During his membership of the Lords two measures which appeared in the 1584–85 session, one concerning revenues from wardship, the other against fraudulent conveyances, were undoubtedly officially inspired. Indeed Elizabeth was said to have described the latter as 'her own bill'. On the other hand, bills which dealt with matters of local, rather

23

than national, concern often originated from outside official circles, for example, from towns anxious to promote their own causes. London was the most obvious and actively organised initiator, though York also regularly promoted bills, and other towns and cities could be counted among those providing business for Parliament.[15] Otherwise we may gain some guidance from the means of differentiation established recently by Professor Elton, namely by looking at the enacting clauses of acts and, where they survive, the bills which failed to become acts. It was his theory that a short enacting clause, which said in effect that the bill was to be enacted by authority of the present Parliament, indicated that there was 'government' origin, while a longer clause which spoke of enactment by the Queen with the advice and consent of the Lords and the Commons and the authority of the same, indicated that non-offical individuals or interest groups had been at work.[16]

The 'test' sometimes produces strange results however, and it cannot be used as an infallible guide, as a measure to limit benefit of clergy in 1576 shows. A short enacting clause indicates a 'government'-inspired bill, yet, as far as we can tell, it owed much of its eventual form to others.[17] In fact, although it seems that the Council often prepared lists of measures either before, or during, sessions, we do not know much about such proposals. When we do, as in 1559 and 1563, the range was fairly comprehensive, from enclosures and bullion export to tutors for peers' children, and from bishops' consecration to benefit of clergy. It is also likely that such planning became more 'modest' as time went on, and that others could produce ideas for legislation, aimed particularly at reforming the administration of the law of the land itself. The key to understanding what often happened when law was made may be seen in the Shoemakers' Act of 1559. This had been envisaged in the 'government plan', but it developed out of discussions between Council and shoemakers, and carried the long, 'unoffical', enacting clause as a result of being drafted by groups concerned.[18] It may not be surprising then that the major act for the Queen's safety in 1584–85 also carried a long enacting clause, even though it arose from deep concern on the part of the Council. *Everyone* was concerned about this matter, and the bill's journey through the Houses – which included redrafting and amendment – makes the long clause (possibly a change along the way) less of a surprise.[19]

The significance of the foregoing is emphasised if we apply the 'enacting clause test' to the legislative output of Elizabeth's parliaments. This shows that 61 per cent of the acts have long clauses, and that 75 per cent of official acts have short clauses. Though these figures need to be viewed cautiously, as we have seen, and though the proportions vary from the first half of the reign to the second, the message is clear. The task of making law in Elizabethan England was one which involved men outside official circles on a considerable scale. This is the most helpful way in which Parliament can be seen as a co-operative venture. The contribution of 'non-government' parties to the product of parliamentary endeavour is considerable and persistent. Indeed, in so far as legislation played an important part in the administration – the governing – of the realm, this important contribution in its turn defines and limits what we conventionally describe as 'the government' itself.[20]

LAWMAKING AND INITIATIVES: THE EXAMPLES OF 1563 AND 1598

The problems associated with the origins of bills and the ways in which they were judged to be acceptable or otherwise may be illustrated by a number of bills and acts from the two sessions of 1563 and 1597–98. These parliaments were concerned with dealing with critical social and economic situations demanding legislative responses. Two measures stand out in the session of 1563, the Tillage Act and the famous Statute of Artificers. The first of these sought to control the extent of conversion of arable land to pasture, and remained on the statute books for nearly thirty years thereafter. The second made extensive stipulations about the terms of apprenticeship and levels of wages. At this time the effects of inflation and famine were of major concern, and a flu epidemic had cut back the population. The regime had undertaken currency reform in 1560–61, and in the interests of stability it seemed appropriate to restate the general policy with regard to the use of land, and to codify existing provision for setting maximum wage levels. The anti-enclosure stance apparent throughout much of the century was therefore confirmed, as was the associated attempt to prevent the decay of houses of husbandry. The act of 1563 was really a codification of existing legislation, intended to reinforce what should have been current practice, and because Cecil seems to have had prior knowledge of the bill's existence, it might be

25

thought that it was 'official', inspired by the Council. Yet the enacting clause does not provide ready confirmation of this: indeed, it is odd that it refers to the bill being 'ordained' rather than 'enacted'. It may be that it derived from a set of articles produced in non-offical circles, and that it had then been drafted in its unusual form after initial discussion with Cecil.[21]

The Statute of Artificers was intended to secure social stability. Its passage now seems to show less of the confusion of purpose once thought to characterise it. The measure set out to provide the means to regulate contracts of service in agriculture and manufacturing, as well as the terms of apprenticeship and wages. Wage regulation would be achieved by means of assessment subject to regular review in the context of local market conditions. It is clear that the substance of the act had first appeared in 1559, where it was on the agenda probably in the form of two bills, one for apprenticeship, and the other for wages. By 1563, the measure combined the two earlier proposals and carried a short enacting clause, therefore suggesting Council or official initiation. The bill then underwent a process of expansion in debate and committee. It is unlikely that older views which suggested private origins for this measure can stand, therefore. Neither does it seem that the apprenticeship clauses were an afterthought, as was once assumed. They were a core concern, even before Parliament opened, and may have been part of a version of a bill already drawn. Progress through the Houses was clearly complicated, and there were both modifications and additions to the bill. Yet it remained in essence an amalgamation of the Council-inspired proposals of 1559. Significantly, however, it is not possible to 'say with confidence what parts of this very long act represent additions or modifications, or even gaps created by deletion'.[22]

On the other hand, the 1563 Poor Relief Act – undoubtedly a measure of social stabilisation – does not seem to have drawn its inspiration immediately from official circles, though the fact that it was a major bill which started its life in the Lords might suggest government initiative. The parishes of England were to administer poor relief, and ecclesiastical sanctions and admonitions were to encourage charitable donations for the poor. Beyond this, it had no great innovatory character. It has been suggested that its provisions indicate that the bishops were prominent in its formulation; but whether an act formulated in such high places can properly be seen as wholly 'unofficial' in Elizabethan England is doubtful.[23] After this act, which had only a limited life and expired in 1571, the problem of divining initiatives in legislation for the poor becomes more complex. It is clear, however, that when what were apparently private initiatives were discussed in the Commons, Privy Councillors were willing to approve of them, even if they had not planned them. In fact they were ready to produce their own constructive ideas. In the course of debate on an unofficially proposed bill in 1571, Knollys proposed a means of financing a general system of support for the poor which later saw the light of day in the law of 1576.[24] The 1571 bill was defeated by the Lords, but formed the basis of the law of 1572, passed as an official measure. This was more ground-breaking because it provided for compulsory levies for the poor, to be enforced by the secular state. By 1576 the Council took a less equivocal lead. It apparently discussed a measure some weeks before Parliament met, and the act which passed stipulated that work be found for those unable to do so themselves. It has long been recognised that the development of the poor law in Elizabethan England owed much to the contribution of local initiatives outside central government, but we can now see that this illustrates the positive interplay of ideas which seems to lie at the heart of much of the legislative output of Parliament, and demonstrates some of the ways in which government worked.[25]

These examples from 1563 seem to show that government or Council responsibility for major legislation could be limited, if only because no one appears to have thought it strange that others should actively participate. This picture is reflected, not surprisingly, in what was probably the largest single group of bills to come before the Houses, namely those relating to manufacture and trade.[26] Many of these bills were clearly the result of the labours of special interest groups. Little evidence of the collective initiative of the Council can be detected here, so that it is hard to see that there was much 'state planning' of the nation's manufacturing industries, as was once thought to be the case. It used to be thought that the legislation of 1563 for the leather industry, which provided a kind of code of protection until well into the seventeenth century, was the result of the Council's consolidation of a number of private initiatives. However, this has been questioned because the act's provisions were hardly realistic, so much so that it has been suggested that the industry only survived by evading the act.[27] This may not in itself constitute a real

27

case for supposing that the Council had not supported and endorsed the bill: Cromwell's attempts to legislate for meat prices in the 1530s may be said to have been equally 'unrealistic'. But the role of the Council in these matters generally does not seem prominent: even in the cloth trade, a major area of manufacturing and export activity, which was affected by chronic depression, it looks as though a multiplicity of local and regional interests dictated the kind of bills attempted, rather than there being an obvious coherent government plan.[28]

What do these examples from 1563 tell us about the nature of 'government', in particular with regard to legislation? England's economy was highly diversified. Its conflicting craft and regional interests would have made a 'master-plan' difficult to conceive, and in any case the lack of a formalised bureaucracy made standardisation and control difficult to contemplate. In some respects moreover, there was a minimal consensus of economic wisdom which many could, and did, subscribe to, thus making a continuing government intervention and supervision almost redundant and unnecessary. So, turning to the Navigation Act of 1563, with its 'unofficial' enacting clause, we see a portmanteau of initiatives and purposes, which has even been described as a confusion. There was, however, an underlying common-sense belief that England's political strength and safety depended in part on the size of her merchant fleet, and that this should be encouraged to grow. The act therefore prescribed that much of our export and import activity should be carried out by English merchantmen, or failing that, taxed at a higher rate. It was regularly renewed well into the next century.[29]

It thus appears that in social and economic matters the official role was often one of accepting, rather than initiating policy as far as legislation was concerned.[30] The important acts for tillage and houses of husbandry which were passed in 1598 may also shed light on the problem of legislative initiative. They also tell us something about the process of judging legislative proposals adopted by men in Parliament. A shortage of corn in the later 1580s was perhaps an early warning that the current policy on enclosure needed reinforcement. A tillage bill made good progress in both houses in 1589, though it did not become an act, and in 1593 earlier legislation limiting conversion to pasture had been repealed because of plentiful grain supplies.[31] By the late 1590s the situation had become worse, and Parliament opened in October 1597 against a background of poor harvests and taxation collection (from 1593) which had only been completed in the spring of the same year. There had also been levies of men for overseas military and naval expeditions in the struggle against Spain, which had not been met with universal enthusiasm. Spates of enclosure, albeit localised, made the need for reform clear, and the infamous Oxfordshire rebellion of 1596 merely reinforced the case. It cast a shadow over proceedings because it seemed to show that, when called upon to act against a threat to good order, the local gentry had not responded well.[32]

It was, therefore, almost inevitable that Parliament would review the state of agriculture and society in 1597. Neale considered that by this later part of the regime the government was showing signs of enfeeblement, though it is interesting that in other fields Burghley's achievements were arguably impressive. The 'government' was weakened, Neale argued, because in earlier sessions it would have taken the lead here, if only because others were 'so absorbed with religious causes that there was little energy for other matters'. In 1597 there was no immediate sign of Burghley's involvement in the legislation on enclosure or on poverty: the bills were framed by committees of the Commons, signifying a weakening of government leadership. Although he considered that commonwealth matters such as these were properly the province of the House, or Houses, Neale went on to assert that a significant stage in 'winning the initiative' had been reached which would effect a constitutional revolution.[33]

This notion of a major constitutional leap is complex, and deserves closer scrutiny. In the first place our knowledge of legislative initiative tells us that enacting clauses are a reasonable guide to the origins of measures: in these two cases, one act, on houses of husbandry, carries the 'official' clause, the other, on tillage, the 'unofficial' clause. Though they grew out of Francis Bacon's original motion for action on 5 November, and may *prima facie* therefore be considered as unofficially inspired, they both underwent redrafting, and it is hard to believe that the act for houses of husbandry was not officially supported. Despite his initial views, Neale himself, reflecting perhaps the uncertainty surrounding the issue of origins, admitted that the acts may have originated in official circles.[34]

Secondly, our view of what the 'government' might properly be expected to do should not be too rigid, and, as we have seen, there are strong grounds for believing that although the Council might have ideas for new legislation throughout the reign, the participation of others was usually significant. Such measures as the Queen or groups of ministers might envisage would constitute a limited list, and would include any taxation proposals, along with other specific measures for maintaining or enhancing revenue, or perhaps a measure for the Queen's safety in one form or another. Moreover, the Houses, properly viewed, were legitimate parts of 'government' in the realm. That must be the logical conclusion to be drawn from Elizabeth's statement in 1571 when she told the Commons to concern themselves with commonwealth matters.[35] Beyond this however, as we have also seen, the 'government' was not noticeably more visible in the social and economic legislative activity of the earlier part of the reign. Neale's vision of sea changes on this issue appears to have been based on a notion of contrasts which do not now seem to have been real. Equally, it is naive to suppose that the religious fervour of the early years simply took up too much energy for the participants to think of anything else. Thomas Norton, on Neale's reckoning at least, was a religious rebel, yet he also managed to comprehend within his parliamentary timetable a host of different activities, including the drafting of bills. The truth of the matter must be that the crisis of 1597 was one which needed the full participation of as many members as possible, for they were the men with the knowledge of what had happened and the responsibilty of having to deal with the aftermath, and it was they who could best tailor the remedy to fit the needs of the moment. The apparent hands-off approach of the 'government' means no more than this, and certainly does not indicate lack of government awareness of the need to deal with the problem.[36]

The central concern of the bill against the decay of tillage was to ensure that there was sufficient land under cultivation to feed the population. The moment had come to prevent excessive conversion to pasture with all the perceived dangers of depopulation and under-employment which accompanied it. Bacon's words about towns being replaced by 'nought but green fields, a shepherd and his dog' must have struck an awesome note in the minds of many members, especially those who had been closely involved in the Oxfordshire troubles. By 21 November a bill for the preservation of tillage was read, its main provision being to secure re-conversion of land then under pasture if it had previously been tilled for a period of twelve years. It also set its face against further conversion of established tillage land. The act which finally emerged was restricted in scope to twenty-three counties, yet the penalties had been sharpened by the Houses. Cecil was particularly annoyed that the border counties of Cumberland and Westmorland were not included: his hope was that labour-intensive tillage here would ensure a supply of manpower for defence of the northern border. Bacon himself is said to have offered a limited welcome to the act which, he said, was 'like the cock' in not punishing past offences while promising remedies for future ones. Neale was cynical about the reaction of the Commons to the measure, which clearly affected many members' economic interests as land-owners, yet it is not easy to see what else the House could have done in the circumstances.[37]

The second reading debate seems to have been concerned with analysing the root of the problem and discussing the likely conse-quences of the proposed remedy. It was applying the fundamental tests of lawmaking which the Lord Keeper enjoined Parliament to apply. The House was willing, moreover, to listen to the case for selective application, so that some counties were to be free from its stipulations. Though it was pointless to attempt to apply it in those areas where it would be useless, inapplicable or harmful, the princi-ple of the measure was to stand elsewhere. The debate thus gave rise to widely contrasting views about the suitability of the proposal. Two speeches which have survived fortunately represent opposing ends of the argument, so we can be fairly confident that the broad nature of the controversy has not escaped us. From an unnamed speaker there was a vigorous and eloquent contribution in favour of the bill, though it needed to be strengthened. Parliament was 'an epitome of the whole realm', the speaker said, and members must take account of the poor. Tillage was good for the soul of man, because it provided work, and therefore drove out idleness; and a supply of soldiers to strengthen the realm would necessarily follow on the enhancement of a fit work-force. Equally, society would be the poorer if the earth were to remain enhanced in the hands of a few, and the poor in consequence were to remain neglected as if they were not part of the body politic.[38]

The bill was opposed by Henry Jackman, who has been seen as a prime example of the self-seeking member anxious to defeat a meas-ure which would have worked to his financial disadvantage. As a cloth merchant, representing the sheep-rearing interest of Wiltshire, his argument is thought to have been predicated on the view that what was bad for woollen cloth could never be good legislation. However, the opposition of such men did not sink the bill, and in so far as the scope of the measure was limited in its passage through the Houses, its curtailment did not obviously follow the lines of argument which Jackman had adopted. The objection he offered was simply that the bill was wholly inappropriate: it could not prevent further escalations in corn prices, which were not in fact caused by too much pasture land and too little arable production. It was the will of God, expressed through bad weather, which had washed away moderate prices. Keep as much land as you would under the plough, he argued, and a wet summer would still send prices high. Jackman went on to assert that the bill was not merely ineffectual. It was positively 'mischievous and inconvenient to the commonwealth'. If the production of wool were restricted, cloth prices would be driven up and unemployment in the woollen cloth industry would ensue. It is against this background that the measure must be judged, for it appears that Parliament saw some merit in the original proposal, though it thought it prudent to limit its coercive powers to those areas where it was practical to compel farmers to resort to tillage. It made little sense generally to force upland areas to engage in what would have been unprofitable grain-growing activities, and as another speaker said on behalf of his own county, the dairy-producing areas of pastureland needed to be allowed to continue as such.[39]

Neale was also surprised that the Commons, dominated as it was by landowners, was apparently willing to attack enclosing landlords in the other measure introduced by Bacon. This was directed against the depopulation which occurred as a result of the demolition of farms. It may be that the numbers of small farms destroyed was not great, but the hard times of the 1590s may have forced some men into insolvency, and the issue exerted an influence powerful enough to produce the act of 1598. The intention was to preserve 'houses of husbandry' from destruction for the sake of land enclosure. Farms with twenty acres, and occupied for at least three years since 1559, were to be kept intact. The bill apparently attracted more whole-hearted support in the Commons than in the Lords, where it under-went redrafting which was eventually accepted after a joint confer-ence between the Houses. Although the act clearly stated that there should be no further reduction in the numbers of houses, the Lords

had scaled down, though not removed, the requirements for rebuild-
ing and re-endowing with land which the Commons had originally
wanted to apply to offenders and their heirs, as well as the purchasers
of such land.[40]

It is important to stress the atmosphere in which the measure was
passed. Depopulation and poverty were at the root of the Oxfordshire
agitation, and the fact that the intentions of a few disorderly subjects
had not been realised was, in a way, the least important part of the
picture. Conspiracy had appeared to reveal the fragility of the social
order, a consideration all the more pointed in the context of the
continued Spanish threat which persisted in these later years of the
reign. The original title of the bill proclaimed its purpose to be 'the
increase of the people for the service and defence of the realm', and it
thus struck a strong patriotic note. Although this was subsequently
changed so as to speak of 'the prevention of decaying of towns and
houses of husbandry', the preamble retained the purpose as set out in
the original title, but also linked it compellingly with the notion that
poverty and vagrancy – the other great preoccupations of the 1597
session – could be controlled by the act:

> Where a good part of the strength of this realm consisteth in the
> number of good and able subjects ... and where of late years, more
> than in times past, there have sundry towns, parishes and houses of
> husbandry been destroyed and become desolate by means whereof a
> great number of poor people are become wanderers, idle and loose,
> which is the causeof infinite inconveniences.

To oppose a bill which was so clearly a measure for the strengthening
and stabilising of the realm was to court ignominy.[41]

A cynical approach, however, is to suggest that it was clear that it
was unnecessary to oppose the passage of the bill. Its enforcement
was dependent on the existing cumbersome machinery of the local
courts. Nothing new was added to strengthen the judicial armoury
throughout England. The problem of law enforcement had been a
well-nigh constant preoccupation of Lords Chancellor and Keeper
throughout the reign. The opening and closing addresses to Parliament had not only spoken of the need for specific law provision and
general legal review, but had commonly emphasised the need, sometimes in barely concealed tones of impatience, for the legislators in
Parliament to see to it that their work was executed when they went
home to their counties and, as Justices of the Peace, became the law-

enforcers. In fact, some of Nicholas Bacon's most elegant parliamentary prose was devoted to this aspect of administration and government. In this light it is worth briefly considering the act itself in order to see where the difficulties of enforcement may have lain.[42]

The act's provisions bristle with statements which appear to provide opportunities for all sorts of exemptions and evasions. For instance, offenders were to rebuild a proportion of houses which had been decayed for more than seven years, and forty acres of land were to be 'laid to them', that is, if the offenders possessed land which was 'fit and convenient' for farming. Who was to determine this, and how, was not specified. The act also said that houses were to be kept in repair by 'occupiers and possessors', though this could act as an obviously prohibitive condition of renting to be operated by the landlord. Any gentleman who had built his own dwelling house and taken up to 120 acres to do so, or two houses of husbandry, in order to maintain hospitality and his own house, was not to be deemed guilty of any offence under the act. The act did not extend to deer parks, or the houses on them. This was only part of an apparatus which suggests an unwieldiness and potential for complications in the legal process which could be protracted, and therefore very expensive. Nor was there any indication in the act as to who would, or could, take action against alleged enclosers.[43]

We are not primarily concerned here with the effectiveness of legislation after it had left Parliament, though in the long run historians will need to make general appraisals of whether Parliament's work was successful, if only because recent arguments that the institution was a lawmaking, rather than a political, body must stand or fall to a degree on such an appraisal. But it is relevant to remind ourselves that if the Depopulation Act dealt in a cumbersome, and perhaps impracticable, way with a problem whose extent was only limited, then the scaled-down enclosure measure was not an obvious success: conversion to pasture continued, resentment built up, and in 1607 it exploded in the Midland Revolt.[44]

Among the tally of Parliamentary acts in Elizabeth's reign there were some which can be said to have emanated from 'government' sources, by which we usually mean that they carried the initiating support of a number of Privy Councillors: in matters of the subsidy, the safety and security of the Crown, and administrative or legal reform this is to be expected. But not all bills were successfully transformed into acts simply because of this pedigree.[45] We have seen some of the failures, and there were others too, for it seems that a high proportion of about a hundred bills surviving for the period 1584–1601 which failed to reach the statute book were officially inspired. The wider implications of this are that, in so far as the administration or government of the realm depended on acts of Parliament, then the Queen and her Council – as a group of officials at least – apparently had a role which was less prominent than that of the government today. Of the public acts passed during the reign slightly fewer than 60 per cent came from official sources.[46] Yet it is not always easy to divide official and unofficial, though it may be that the divisions were less important to Elizabethans than we might suppose. This is clearly the way in which the co-operative nature of parliamentary endeavour which historians of the period have been keen to emphasise recently has a real and practical meaning. It would appear that making and reviewing of laws was a function of the 'government' of England, in the broader sense, which was assembled in Parliament. These men who gathered there were not surprisingly concerned with their ability to understand the measures they were considering, and with notions of fairness and practicability which could affect them, either as enforcers of law or as those upon whom it was enforced. It is likely that they were also driven sometimes by more self-seeking considerations, and by a desire to cover themselves in the protective shroud of the law against the potential threat of an over-demanding monarch.[47] On the other hand, we must remember how important were practical considerations in deciding the outcome of debate and the fate of bills. The consequence of this may be seen in other areas too, for it must modify any tendency to see religious debate, for example, solely in terms of a rigidified divide between Protestant and Catholic. This may help to explain the outcome of some episodes which have puzzled some historians in the past (see Chapter 5).

NOTES

1 See Graves, *Tudor Parliaments*, p. 2.

2 *Procs.*, p. 47.

3 See Chapter 5; *Procs.*, pp. 339–40, 502–8; *EP*, i.385–92.

4   *Procs.*, p. 35.

5   *Procs.*, pp. 83, 183.

6   D'Ewes, *Journals*, p. 524; USA Huntington Library, Ellesmere MS 2569; cf. Graves, *Elizabethan Parliaments*, pp. 62–5 on this.

7   *Procs.*, pp. 448–51, 454–6; *EP*, i.354–6; *PE*, pp. 271–3, 284–6.

8   *Procs.*, pp. 448–51.

9   *Procs.*, p. 203; see Chapter 3.

10 *PE*, pp. 191–4.

11 *PE*, pp. 231–2.

12 *PE*, p. 256.

13 Graves, *Elizabethan Parliaments*, pp. 58–60; *PE*, Chapter 5.

14 Graves, *Elizabethan Parliaments*, p. 70; *PE*, pp. 51–2; Dean, 'Enacting clauses', p. 141.

15 *PE*, pp. 71, 76–86, 93; *EP*, ii.84, 91; Dean, 'Enacting clauses', pp. 142–3.

16 Elton, *Studies in Tudor and Stuart Politics*, iii.142–55.

17 *PE*, pp. 63–6, 67.

18 *PE*, pp. 71–2, 74.

19 Dean, 'Enacting clauses', p. 143 and n.25.

20 Dean, 'Enacting clauses', p. 141; n. b. Graves, *Elizabethan Parliaments*, pp. 64–5.

21 Palliser, *Age of Elizabeth*, pp. 150–1; *PE*, pp. 229–30.

22 *PE*, pp. 262–7.

23 *PE*, pp. 267–8.

24 *Procs.*, p. 219.

25 *PE*, pp. 269–71; Slack, *Poverty in Tudor and Stuart England*, p. 124.

26 *PE*, p. 235.

27 *PE*, pp. 246–7.

28 Lehmberg, *Reformation Parliament*, pp. 173 and n.2; Elton, *Reform and Renewal*, p. 111; *PE*, p. 249.

29 *PE*, pp. 258–62.

30 *PE*, p. 262.

31 Palliser, *Age of Elizabeth*, pp. 183–4.

32 Williams, *Tudor Regime*, p. 182; MacCulloch, *Suffolk and the Tudors*, p. 282 for constitutional opposition to government requests for assistance;

Manning, *Village Revolts*, pp. 221–9; Walter, 'A "rising of the people"?'.

33 Read, *Lord Burghley and Queen Elizabeth*, pp. 531–3; *EP*, pp. 332–3, 337.

34 Dean, 'Enacting clauses', pp. 144–5.

35 *Procs.*, p. 199.

36 See Fox and Guy, *Reassessing the Henrician Age*, p. 161 for Cromwell the author against Cromwell the architect: would evidence that the 'government' sponsored these bills in 1597 prove that they were there own, rather than adoptions?

37 *EP*, pp. 339, 344–5.

38 Hatfield MS 176, fos. 11–12; *EP*, ii.339–41.

39 BL Lansdowne MS 105, fos. 201–3; 83, fo. 198.

40 Palliser, *Age of Elizabeth*, p. 184; *EP*, ii.345–7.

41 *SR*, iv.891.

42 See, for example, *Procs.*, e.g. pp. 49–51, 72, 82–4; Thirsk, *Agrarian History of England*, iv.229–31.

43 *SR*, iv.891–3.

44 Palliser, *Age of Elizabeth*, p. 184.

45 See *PE*, pp. 242–4 for armaments.

46 Dean, 'Enacting clauses', pp. 141, 148 and n.59.

47 *PE*, p. 258.

Chapter 3

Taxation and royal finance

Our knowledge of the reasons for granting taxes and the parliamentary process involved is far better than it was ten years ago. It is clear that Henry VIII managed to obtain large grants of taxation, some of which were levied in peacetime. It was not necessary to justify taxation as a means of paying for the extraordinary expense of war. Even though some historians have rejected the notion that Elizabeth's parliaments were political and constitutional battlegrounds, a feeling persists that tax demands caused resentment and difficulties. An examination of various aspects of parliamentary subsidies sheds valuable light on this subject. Along with other areas of royal finance, it also yields important clues about parliamentary perspectives on, and expectations of, Elizabeth's rule.[1]

At the beginning of every reign the two Houses of Parliament agreed to grant the monarch the traditional customs duties of tonnage and poundage. This was accomplished by an act of 1559 and was the legal basis for Elizabeth's levying of the duties from the start of her reign in November 1558 until she died in 1603.[2] Little is known at present of the clerical subsidies which were granted by Convocation sitting simultaneously with Parliament, but in two respects at least it differs from what we know of the lay subsidy. In the first place, the bill by which Parliament acknowledged Convocation's grant was introduced, not into the Commons, but into the Lords, where it was offered by the Archbishop of Canterbury as leader of the clerical estate sitting in the Upper House. This might happen half-way through a session, and progress through the two Houses was very quick. Like the lay subsidy acts, the clerical subsidy legislation demonstrated a preoccupation with the necessity for defence of the realm, and with the glorification of the Queen's merits and virtues. Secondly, the yields from taxing the clergy appear to have increased as the reign progressed, though the maximum yield was less than £20,000 a year. However, together with with the customs duties, including tonnage and poundage, which also yielded greater returns to the Crown at the end of the reign, clerical taxation must be counted a success story in comparison with the lay subsidy. This, as we shall see, was producing smaller returns for the Queen in her later years.[3]

THE PARLIAMENTARY SUBSIDY

It was, however, the lay subsidy, together with the fifteenth and tenths, which most concerned Parliament on a regular basis. On 25 January 1559, Lord Keeper Bacon's address to Elizabeth's first assembly announced in broad terms the long-term objectives of the Queen's reign. If religion could be established soundly, the commonwealth would be securely based and stability ensured. Continual change and alteration would thus be avoided 'as things much to be eschewed'. A substantial part of his reported oration was concerned with taxation, and this was, with the exception of the 1572 session alone, a regular request made of the Queen's subjects. In this long address, Bacon stressed Elizabeth's extensive virtues. There were many reasons for men to be joyous, he said, though at the same time there was occasion for sadness because Elizabeth had ascended a throne whose resources were depleted. 'Could there have happened to this imperial Crown a greater loss in honour, strength and treasure than to lose that piece, Calais I mean, which in the beginning was so nobly won ...? Did not the keeping of this breed fear to our mightiest enemies and make our faint friends the more assured ...?' There had also been a substantial loss of artillery, of Crown and subjects' revenue, and of manpower, and there were debts to be paid at 'biting' levels of interest. The enormous cost of defending the realm against further losses by strengthening the navy and the garrisons of the land had to be contemplated. We should not, however, despair, said Bacon, for any man who gave a moment's thought to this would surely 'adventure land, limb, yea and life' so as to prevent further decay and promote recovery. It was necessary that every individual should assent to the granting of financial assistance, and 'every one particularly should ... concur and join to relieve and assist the whole universally'.[4]

The Lord Keeper – or Lord Chancellor if Elizabeth had appointed one – made similar speeches whenever a new parliament was opened. Otherwise a member of the Council sitting in the Commons, like Sir Walter Mildmay, would initiate the matter when a prorogued parliament reassembled. Sometimes, as in 1563 and 1571, a member outside official circles started the process, but the Councillors were never far away with supporting speeches if they had not actually initiated the matter themselves.[5] Whether it was in time of peace or war, to cover past expenditure – for example, the French and Scottish ventures in 1563 – or for the later struggle against Spain, Elizabeth's ministers were asking for financial assistance for the preservation of the commonwealth. Thus there were twelve requests in the long reign, and twelve subsidy acts resulted. When Bacon spoke in 1559 he clearly had an eye on future provision as well as paying for past expenditure, for he emphasised the need for strong garrisons to defend the borders. A disastrous war had weakened and financially stretched the Crown, he said, and this had also to be set against the enemy's strength: 'how ready he is upon every occasion, upon every side, and in every time to annoy you'. The Subsidy Act which resulted also reflected the notion of providing for the future when it spoke of the need 'to be ready against all occurrences'. Later on, in 1576, Sir Walter Mildmay's request for a subsidy may have made the notion of further provision, rather than simply meeting earlier expenses, more explicit. The 1576 Subsidy Act certainly spoke of the need to prevent 'mischiefs before they break into open flame' as well as quenching them 'when once kindled'. It is hard to see that this amounted to the adoption of a 'whole new tack by the government in its relations with parliament' for the underlying theme was apparent at the outset in what Bacon said. The Elizabethan regime was to be preserved for as long as possible.[6]

Traditionally, a single subsidy was granted. This was a tax on land or goods which was meant to reflect the wealth of the payee, and therefore involved assessment of income. The onset of open war with Spain meant that the single subsidy became inadequate, and it had to be multiplied. In 1589 therefore, the grant became a double subsidy, and the last parliament of the Queen's reign agreed to a contribution of four subsidies for the expensive and protracted war.[7] Parliament, which in Henry's reign was willing to grant subsidies, even though some might argue that his spending in later years was reckless, apparently continued a tradition of amenability and co-operativeness. The language of the statutes seems to confirm this, for it was generally fulsome in its expression of loyalty to the Queen. The Statute of 1563, for example, expressed the subjects' thanks to God for the great felicity shown to them by his preservation of Elizabeth, whom they were ready to serve with all obeisance and loyalty 'to the uttermost of our power, and end of our lives'.[8]

Sometimes there may have been minor disagreements about the technicalities of getting the bill from one House to the other, but generally there were no real problems over the subsidy as such. On the face of it therefore, there was a good deal of co-operation on this issue between Queen and subjects represented in Parliament. The point has been emphasised recently if only to dismiss the suggestion that parliamantary taxation could cause trouble between the Queen and the Commons.[9] Some historians have been inclined to think that requests for money, which were a principal reason in the Queen's mind for calling Parliament, caused resentment in themselves. More than this, it was possible that they were used to compel her to react favourably to parliamentary petitions on a variety of subjects. However, even those who believed that Elizabethan parliamentary history was a confrontation between Commons and Queen did not argue that there was much friction over the incidence and multiplication of the subsidy, or that it was used *extensively* as a lever to extract concessions on other matters. It is important then to determine how far the Queen and her subjects were able to co-operate in this area, if only because it was for her the most important reason for summoning Parliament.[10]

Part of the problem of understanding parliamentary attitudes to the subsidy is that there is little evidence of debate.[11] The Subsidy Bill's progress was often protracted over a number of weeks, though this did not necessarily indicate difficulty over the proposal itself, or that it was used as a lever on other issues. In 1581, although there were no apparent difficulties, almost five weeks elapsed from start to finish in the Commons, though less than three weeks were needed in 1584–85. In 1601 – when the monopolies question was also on the agenda – the bill passed the Commons in four and a half weeks.[12] Taking time over the Subsidy Bill – weeks rather than days – was a recognised way of prolonging the session, however, or at least ensuring that it would not end quickly.[13] In the meantime, other legislative activity could proceed. The fears of members, such as Mr Wingfield in 1601, that Parliament would end before much lawmaking could be achieved once the subsidy had been passed, could thus be allayed.[14] In itself, the subsidy may not have occupied a disproportionate amount of the Houses' time or been problematic at all, but because the bill took weeks rather than days to complete its passage, and other matters were being dealt with along the way, it could easily appear that progress was not only 'slow' but had been deliberately 'slowed' as a tactical weapon. It is also hard to be certain about motivation. It is possible to see deliberate delay in 1601, though ensuring there was adequate time for discussion of monopolies, rather than forcing the Queen's hand may have been the explanation.[15] It remains true, however, that money was granted when asked for, a principled unwillingness to grant supply is barely recorded, and when the Subsidy Bill was used tactically, it was other than a bald threat to withhold financial assistance to the Crown. While there may be no real evidence that the lay subsidy was consistently regarded as a tactical weapon, it took its place in a scheme of things where parliamentary sessions were seen, though not always by the Queen, as serving ends other than merely granting her the wherewithal to tax men up and down the nation.[16]

SUBSIDIES AND POLITICAL CONFRONTATION

The process of granting taxation had to take its place alongside other parliamentary business, and the 1566 session provides a good example of the problems which could arise as a result, both for contemporary Elizabethans and for historians. The desire to persuade the Queen to name a successor – a desire shared by all, as we shall see – appeared on 18 October when John Molyneux urged that the House revive 'the suit for succession and to proceed with the subsidy'; this was the day after Sir Edward Rogers and Sir William Cecil had introduced the question of the subsidy. We cannot be sure what Molyneux had in mind here, and whether he specifically wanted the subsidy witheld unless action on the succession was forthcoming.[17] Moreover, a copy of an anonymous speech, which may have been Molyneux's own, can also be interpreted in different ways, though he did say that he had prepared a bill which offered a subsidy and which tried 'to obtain her Majesty's loving, willing and favourable consent unto this weighty cause'.[18] If this was an attempt at a strategic use of the Subsidy Bill, Molyneux must be considered rashly optimistic if he wanted, as has been suggested, to get the subsidy business successfully launched so that the question of the succession could then be raised. Perhaps he thought Elizabeth would look kindly on Parliament's wishes on the succession once she had the assurance of her money. The evidence is unclear therefore, though the issue of the succession could have been seen as giving the subsidy a potential strategic importance in a number of ways rather than being a simple *quid pro quo*.[19]

Merely linking the two issues could have been tantamount, however, to pressure on the Queen, and Sir Ralph Sadler's speech, apparently made in answer to Molyneux, spelled this out clearly enough.[20] We should not, he said, 'mix and mingle' the succession with the matter of the subsidy, for it would look as though we were trying to 'condition and covenant' with her Majesty. His own solution was to pray to God, advice which Elizabeth herself would surely have applauded. Here was an occasion when the Commons could scarcely avoid being menacing from Elizabeth's point of view. The coincidence of the subsidy with the highly sensitive issue of the succession, left over from 1563, meant that it was inevitable as soon as Molyneux's intervention made it explicit. Withholding supply – if that had been the intention – would be a threat, but offering it could appear to be blackmail, a point not lost on Elizabeth herself. She was alleged to have told the Spanish ambassador that Parliament wanted to buy her acquiescence for a quarter of a million pounds. The Queen's famous remission of part of the proposed grant can hardly be seen as other than a reflection of the political difficulties she faced at this time. It might have been a symbolic distancing of herself from what she considered to be money tainted because it was meant to buy progress on the succession. On the other hand, Elizabeth felt she needed to mend fences because the succession matter had impinged explosively on the question of the liberties of the Commons (see Chapter 4). Her gesture at this point was later used as an example of her gracious and lenient treatment of her subjects. She had summoned Parliament in order to raise money, and then given part of it back before it was even collected, a startling demonstration of generous-hearted regality.[21]

The question of the sovereignty of the Netherlands which arose in 1586–87 was perhaps the most interesting example of an attempt to use taxation, or an additional money grant (a benevolence) in this case, as a means of inducing the Queen to follow a particular policy line. It also nicely illustrates other aspects of parliamentary taxation which arose on other occasions. The call for financial help from this Parliament gave Job Throckmorton, one of the most fiercely patriotic speakers in the Commons, the opportunity to urge Elizabeth to assume the sovereignty of the Netherlands. This would stiffen local resistance to Spain, and so ward off the militant Catholicism many feared would, in turn, threaten England. In unfolding his message in the House, Throckmorton displayed a virulent suspicion and mistrust not only for Spain, but for the French, and James of Scotland himself, who must by now have been regarded as the prospective king of England following his mother's recent execution. This alone would not have pleased Elizabeth, for at a time of increased tension with Spain, she was clearly banking on good relations with both Scotland and France. Throckmorton was also convinced that God yearned for her to reform her Church as part of a grand scheme to strengthen the realm. For Throckmorton, as for others, Elizabeth's England was a precious jewel, and part of his conviction that this was so derived from an arrogant confidence that God was English himself.[22]

Privy Councillors in the Commons could hardly have been happy about the undiplomatic quality of this speech, though there cannot be any real doubt about their wish that the Queen should intervene more actively in the Netherlands. Mildmay himself, the Chancellor of the Exchequer, appears to have led the Commons committee firmly in the direction of considering a benevolence over and above the subsidy as the best means of financing action which would follow on the assumption of sovereignty by Elizabeth. However, he was careful to stress that the decision on the matter would be hers alone. Knollys also emphasised the political niceties of the situation, though neither of these responsible men can have had any doubt that Elizabeth would regard the mere occurrence of debate of this kind as abhorrent. Neither can Speaker Puckering have failed to see the same when he noted that the Commons would be willing to promise additional money if the sovereignty were assumed. Convocation's wish to grant an additional benevolence of its own put further pressure on the Queen, though the Church did not link sovereignty with it. It is doubtful, however, if Councillors and other members would have agreed that the monarchy 'was in danger' as a result of their action. After their arguments failed, they had no means of compelling the Queen to their favoured line of action. Elizabeth's command to proceed no further can have been no surpise.[23]

In this episode the question of finance was intimately linked with the Queen's own determination of policy. She seems to have been at odds with leading subjects on the important subject of the safety of the realm. The issue was not entirely clear-cut, however, and realism shaped the views of some fervent Protestants like James Morice. He wondered whether it was feasible to demand that the subject pay a tax *and* a benevolence, and the Commons' decision ultimately reflected this caution. The benevolence, if granted, would fall only on the shoulders of the wealthier subject. Such scruples were of no concern to Elizabeth, however. The Commons' offer was spurned, as was that of the Lords, who had been careful to keep theirs separate from that of the Lower House, even though Sir Francis Knollys suggested provocatively that the two Houses join hands in offering this financial inducement.[24]

Another occasion on which it looks as though political pressure was exerted through the subsidy came in 1601, when the bill was apparently held up until progress on the monopolies issue was made in the House. By this stage, however, the Commons had already agreed to the unprecedented demand of four subsidies, and the discussion had been concerned not with whether or not the subsidies should be granted, but how they were to be levied, and how the burden should be spread between rich and poor. Perhaps the desire to press on with monopolies was the most urgent consideration in members' minds, and the refusal to proceed with the Subsidy Bill at the second reading stage was because it was seen as an unwelcome distraction. It could be argued, then, that tactical considerations about monopolies had their impact on the business of granting supply, though there is no evidence that the grant itself was jeopardised. As the Queen's intention to end the session before Christmas had been made clear at the outset, it is easy to understand a developing sense of impatience in some members by the end of November simply because nothing had yet been decided about monopolies.[25]

There is thus a suggestion, at least, that members were aware of the potential for using the Crown's financial needs as a means towards other ends, but it is hard to see outright opposition to it in its own right, or a willingness to use supply as part of an overall strategy of confrontation and opposition. We need to be careful, however, about what conclusions we draw from this.

It is important therefore to return to the wider context of taxation. The topic was often aired initially on the first day of the elaborate procedural opening ceremony. It was argued that it was a necessary means of protecting England, and government spokesmen from time to time waxed lyrical about the constant threat to English shores. The 'waves of the sea do one follow upon another without intermission', said Mildmay in 1585, and in 1597 the need was to avoid 'the forces and invasions of the king of Spain'.[26] In 1601, the young member Hayward Townshend reported that Cecil drove the point home when he spoke of the threats to the Queen's life, and how Ireland had been breached by Spanish forces. Cecil said he had seen the jewels at Elizabeth's waist which had been given to would-be assassins as the price for her life, a chilling reminder of how slender was the thread upon which England's good fortune depended. The obvious and repeated patriotic purpose of parliamentary taxation renders it hard to envisage how there could have been anything like a sustained determination to deny the Queen financial assistance. Her request for money was patently not for her own selfish benefit and in an age of inflation, Scottish and French ventures in the early years, internal rebellion in 1569 and intermittent war for the whole of the second half of her reign the Crown's own resources were under serious strain and needed reinforcement.[27]

A willingness to grant subsidies was an expression of co-operative solidarity, and could serve as a propaganda weapon against the enemy. In 1601 Robert Cecil was anxious that Spain should realise that Englishmen were willing to be taxed to the extremity of having to sell their pots and pans, even though he was keen to argue later that he did not imagine that this would actually have to happen. It was not sensible to display a nation divided in Parliament by grudging attitudes to raising the money to keep it safe. It is easy to understand therefore that most members would be willing enough to complete the process of passing the Subsidy Act, and that if there were dissenting voices they would be rare. One such man found his voice in 1589 apparently, though he was careful to define his objections and to state specifically that the Queen did indeed have a right to taxation, and her subjects a duty to pay.[28]

SUBSIDIES AND RELATED PROBLEMS

While the tactical use of taxation for other political ends may not have been highly developed, and while the national interest guaranteed acceptance of the Crown's requests, we must not assume that the subsidy always enjoyed trouble-free passage. In fact qualms were voiced over a number of issues: the manner of *raising* the tax, the impact on the poor, and the amounts to be levied. What eventually came in to the Exchequer may also have reflected a practical reticence, if not opposition, to what had been demanded. Parliament did not obviously pursue the means to *ease* the raising of taxes. Problems arose in 1563, apparently on the question of whether to retain the oath which the 1559 act had required assessors to swear. That act said that they should be bound to investigate wealth to the 'uttermost substance and values ... without concealment, love, favour, affection, dread, fear or malice'. The act of 1563 stated that the assessors were to be charged 'other than by corporal oath' to enquire of the best and most value of the substance of every person, though the rest of their obligation was formulated in exactly the same words as was the former statute, and a penalty of £10 maximum for failure to do so was introduced. The problem was not so much granting the tax, but how it was going to be administered.[29] It also looks as though members were careful not to suggest that the subject would pay more than was necessary. In 1566 the Queen's renunciation of part of the usual subsidy grant was welcomed, but expressing thankful loyalty in the intended preamble to the Subsidy Act raised eyebrows. The impression had been given, some felt, that an excessive readiness to pay up had been implied.[30]

It has been suggested that the opposition to continuing the oath in 1563 came from 'Puritan' conscientious objections to oath-taking.[31] Whatever the case, the practical effect of its removal was surely foreseeable, even though a fine replaced the oath as a sanction against officials' slackness. The removal of the possibility of a charge of perjury can hardly have promised improved subsidy yields, even though in this particular case the tax floor was reduced from £5 to £3 on goods, so that more men were ostensibly liable to taxation. It is apparent therefore that members of Parliament, who most obviously represented the gentry and provided tax assessors, were controlling the tax-gathering potential of the Crown. The parliaments of Eliza-

beth could easily afford to indulge themselves in statements of patriotic generosity, at least on the statute books. There may have been a
cynical calculation which induced men to agree to tax demands which
increased as the reign wore on, though what materialised actually
declined.

England was not taxed on a massive scale, if only because wealthy
men did not contribute what they could realistically afford. No one
has ever paid taxes willingly, but in Elizabethan England the foot-
dragging was well developed, and widely acknowledged to be so. The
Queen herself was said in 1589 to be so concerned that she was
considering a personal examination of the problem.[32] The well-
known unwillingness of the aristocracy and gentry to assess themselves at realistic levels of wealth had profound effects upon the state
of the royal finances. Though the Queen's financial management has
often been judged conservative and unimaginative, she nevertheless
made great headway in her own finances. The peace which had
prevailed for much of the first half of the reign meant that by the early
1580s the Crown, far from being in debt, had built up some credit
balance. War with Spain obviously undermined this, but even so,
after huge expenditure Elizabeth left a debt of only about a third of a
million pounds to James I. When we consider that the Queen herself
paid for much of the war effort, however, the cost of the achievement
begins to be apparent, and the assumptions and expectations of her
governors stand revealed in sharp contrast. In 1593 Cecil told the
Commons that the double subsidy granted in 1589 had yielded
£280,000 over four years, though Elizabeth, he claimed, had spent
almost four times as much herself, namely £1,030,000. While the
Queen may have received about £104,000 on average each year after
1588 from lay taxation, this only represented an increase of about 10
per cent on the amounts Henry VIII collected in the 1540s, hardly
enough to repair the losses accruing in real terms from inflation. The
yield from individual subsidies was actually falling, both as a figure,
and in real terms because of inflation. Although her own income
from lands had increased by about a quarter during the reign, her
sales of lands meant that this was merely a third of what she might
have gained had she kept them in her own hands.[33] The Queen who
fought a war reluctantly for the last eighteen years of her reign
preserved the lives and lands of her subjects at great cost to herself,
while others were able to see out the years of threat at the price of

relatively low direct taxation. When her leading ministers spoke of her refusal to spend money on vain buildings and pomp and ceremony, they were expressing more than the mere formalities of loyal gratitude. Though these gentlemen may have felt on many occasions that their hopes were frustrated by the Queen, it is hard to see how she can be argued to have got the better of them financially.[34]

Members of the Commons were also willing sometimes to ensure that other means of raising Crown revenue came under scrutiny. Crown officials and commissioners could be guilty of inefficiency at best or corruption at worst. The danger was not only that the Queen was denied what was hers, but that the subject, especially the propertied subject, was being harassed, and that more money than was necessary was demanded. The story of the alleged misconduct of the purveyors – those men commissioned to provision the royal household by purchase of goods at discounted rates in the localities – was already a long one by the time Elizabeth came to the throne. Under the impact of inflationary times and the Queen's needs in wartime, the matter came into sharper focus in this period. In the long run the answer was to substitute what was, in effect, a local rate for what had been a loosely structured system of purveyance. In the meantime attempts at careful statutory control of the purveyors – involving an apparently complex system of checks on their activities – had obviously failed to solve the problem. As a result unscrupulous purveyors had been able to take the opportunity to exploit the situation, for instance, by buying more than was required by the Crown.[35]

Purveyance was part of a general concern voiced by a number of prominent members of the Commons in 1571. Three prominent lawyers, Robert Bell, John Popham and William Lovelace – all of whom were to advance to higher office under the Queen – raised a number of issues, including purveyance. This had appeared in 1563 in the shape of a bill designed to control the practice, but Elizabeth would not agree to statutory control of part of her prerogative powers, and the act failed.[36] Bell, who was to become Speaker in 1572, spoke of the abuses of purveyors as well as the holders of royal licences – the early monopolists – and made a clear connection between this situation and the willingness of the population to pay the subsidy. The Queen would not be able to levy taxes effectively, he seemed to be saying, because of inefficiency and corruption among her own officers. Popham also drew attention to collectors of royal revenue, some of whom deprived the Queen of what was lawfully hers by their fraudulent practices, so that she was consequently compelled to ask for more money in taxes. Lovelace called for a rationalisation of purveyance. He also wanted to reform the activities of Exchequer officials who were thought to pester and harass gentlemen over matters such as distraint of knighthood and respite of homage, and who also probed their landholdings by enquiry into their titles with the writ *quo titulo ingressus est*. Such practices were particularly irksome because the officers were able to levy fees for the execution of the process.[37]

These speakers thus linked the problem of taxation with scrutiny of royal finances on a wide-ranging scale. Even though taxation yields were perhaps smaller than they might to have been, they were nevertheless arguing that the demands were higher than ought strictly to be necessary. It was this need to view the whole picture systematically so as to maximise financial benefit to the Queen which also formed a central concern of Sir Henry Knyvett's speeches on the subsidy in 1593. Here the cry was not that taxes should not be paid, but that the royal revenues as a whole should be scrutinised and maximised, and and he also wanted a nation-wide wealth assessment, followed by a levy which would yield £100,000 to the Queen annually. Massive revaluation must have appeared a threatening prospect, but Sir Walter Raleigh's objection was ingenious. Some men were already over-assessed, he said, and if the truth emerged in a new assessment, their creditworthiness 'which is now their wealth, would be nothing worth'.[38]

Elizabeth was naturally sensitive to any attempt to scrutinise her own finances, and when purveyance emerged for the last time in 1589, along with the problem of the Exchequer officials, she was ready to protect her prerogative. This was, incidentally, one of the sessions when the subsidy may have become part of the strategic thinking of the members. The Subsidy Bill received its second reading in the Commons on 27 February 1589, and the next day it was stated that further progress had been delayed so that others could contribute to the debate. The other reason was that 'some other necessary bills for the commonwealth might be better treated of and expedited in the meantime before the said bill of subsidy ... were prepared so ready to the passing, upon their conjectural opinions that when the subsidy bill were once passed the House the end of this session of parliament was like to ensue shortly after'. We do not know which 'other necessary bills' were envisaged here, but purveyance and Exchequer officials were on the agenda, having appeared as bills on the 14 February, before the Subsidy Bill had been drafted. Delaying the Subsidy Bill may have been seen as a way of ensuring enough time to air the matter fully, even if it remained unlikely that the Queen would allow any bills to go forward. In fact, by 6 March Elizabeth had promised an inquiry into both purveyance and Exchequer officials, four days before the Subsidy Bill received its third reading in the House on 10 March. Before the session ended, the Queen had also apparently promised to involve a number of members in each of these enquiries: purveyance disappeared from the parliamentary agenda after 1589.[39]

In this connection, another worrying aspect of levying subsidies emerged as the reign progressed. This was the question of the poor, and whether frequent and increasing tax demands would be bearable. Already in 1563 more men had been brought into the taxpaying bracket when the point at which tax liability on began was reduced to £3, but thirty years later the '£3 men' had become a worry. In hard times the tax burden on the poorer subject was highlighted, especially as richer men were not taxed adequately. At least some members appear to have recognised that the poor constituted a problem, but, as we have seen in 1601 Cecil adhered to the view, as a public relations weapon at least, that poverty should be no bar to taxpaying at an equal rate throughout society, contrary to the opinion of some who wanted lower rates to apply to the '£3 men'. The concept of the poor taxpayer seemed to be almost a quintessential expression of English patriotism.[40] In 1589, however, one speaker – and one of the few members known to have *opposed* a subsidy grant – had focused on the danger of taxing the poor excessively. Since the country's danger was not evident, he said, it was not clear that taxation was necessary, and if the proposal went ahead it would strain the 'affection' of the Queen's subjects: rebellion and sedition were clear possibilities. He declared that he and his colleagues should consider the poor 'for whom we do sit here more principally than for ourselves'. By this point the view had appeared, though we cannot tell how extensively, that taxation was a potentially divisive element in society, and for that reason it was a large and crucial element in this speaker's objection that it be demonstrated that the need to tax was absolute and clear.[41]

Fears of rebellion also emerged in 1593. Fulke Greville expressed doubts about the wisdom of piling too much on the poor, especially when, as he said, conspicuous consumption and expenditure emphasised the gap between what the rich paid and what they could afford. The dearth of goods – the fact that they could command high prices – was a good indicator that money was in good supply. He warned members that the poor should be helped otherwise they would 'complain'.[42] The Privy Council clearly suspected that wealthy men were indeed under-assessing themselves at the expense of 'persons of the meaner sort'.[43] Burghley claimed that no one in London of all places had been assessed at over £200, and there were fewer than ten men rated between £100 and £200. This appeared to be exaggeration, for Sir John Hart was able to refute the claim easily, showing that fifty-three men had been set at £200 or more, and no less than 148 at between £100 and £200. This must have given the impression that the administration was keen to suppress the real yield it was getting.[44] It also appeared to confirm the view that more sophisticated ways of taxing the rich were necessary to solve the problem in the long term. Mildmay had already suggested in 1581 that taxation was 'easily borne', yet he said it had only paid for half the Queen's 'extraordinary' expenses; and in 1584 he too had complained about wealthy Londoners.[45] If he were to tell memebers how under-assessed the rich were, he said, they would marvel at it. 'Thereby a very great deal less than is given to her Majesty than is paid into her coffers.' But he was not making the point, he said, as a prelude to enhancing 'men's taxations, but to let you see that subsidies thus favourably rated come short of that which you may think'. Sir John Fortescue, the Chancellor of the Exchequer, pointed out that the £3 men made up 50 per cent of the taxpaying population, and he could not therefore accept suggestions which would have led to their exemption from payment. This refusal to alter the basis of taxation was striking because Fortescue recognised the inadequacy of the total yield. While the proposed three subsidies of 1593 were a 'liberal grant', he said, it would not pay for everything, even when the customs revenues had been added. The inefficient, even unjust, current situation was to remain.[46]

There was thus little reason to doubt that subsidy legislation would emerge from any parliamentary session where it had been requested. Even if the measure appeared to get caught up in other matters there was no real problem. To this extent subsidies were regular evidence of the co-operation between Queen and subject in Parliament, though as we have seen, while the outcome was in no doubt, the *process* was no mere formality. The recognised need to pass legislation for taxation did not guarantee that Elizabeth was able to tap the nation's wealth effectively or realistically.[47]

The speeches which initiated the subsidy business assumed something of a regular format, though they were by no means mere formality. Their contents say much about the political and religious frame of mind prevailing in Elizabethan parliaments. The ideas were simple enough, and they were meant to be overwhelmingly compelling. If Englishmen wished to retain what they held so dear, sacrifices would have to be made, even, on occasions, in peacetime. Yet as Bacon asked, was there anyone so mad that, having a whole row of houses in danger from fire, he would not gladly pull some down in order to stop the flames from destroying all? Taken as a whole the speeches in support of the request for subsidies amount in effect to an Elizabethan Protestant creed. The language and ideas which form them, and which were substantially echoed and reinforced in the enactments themselves, deserve more attention because they are clear statements of the way Englishmen thought of the Queen's regime and its purpose.[48]

All too often these sources have been plundered by historians to comment on the notion of war taxation, or peacetime taxation, or taxation for extraordinary expenses both in peacetime or war.[49] It is important, however, to recognise in the first place that a distinction was made in Elizabeth's reign between the *need* for taxation and the *reasons* for it. As Bacon said in 1571, it was necessary in considering the proposed grant of 'extroaordinary' relief to reflect both on the benefits received from Elizabeth's reign and the necessity of the grant. If the second were to be forgotten it would make us seem 'uncareful of our own livings and liberties'. So the rebellious earls in 1569, the war with Spain, and so on, produced a need for money, but the reason for the tax was the very *raison d'être* of the State and the Crown itself, and that involved the subjects' rights and livelihoods.[50] The language of taxation is, in short, much more political than is often realised, and it is connected with a major concern of lawmaking which was a tangible product of parliamentary endeavour, namely the maintenance of property rights.[51]

For much of the reign the sense of deliverance from the 'perils' of Mary Tudor's reign and the need to prevent Catholic invasion informed a major part of thought which was embodied in the preambles. Bacon had made the point of contrast between the reigns clear enough by stressing that Elizabeth would do nothing to advance the cause or quarrel of any foreign power to the destruction of her own subjects. Their preservation, along with that of their homes and families, was her guiding concern. While the first subsidy enactment of the reign spoke of the need to restore and, 'if need be to recover further' the diminished strength and glory of the Crown's former estate', thereafter an 'Elizabethan perspective' had been established. Peace and true religion were the hallmarks of the regime, and it was peace by which 'we generally and joyfully possess all', as Bacon said in 1571. 'No prince has had his hands so clean from blood.' In particular, the speech with which Mildmay opened the subsidy discussions in 1576 presented the case in a nutshell:

> the justice of the realm is preserved and ministered to her people by her Majesty's political and just government ... as our enemies are driven to confess that justice, which is the band of all commonwealths, doth so link together all degrees of persons within this land as there is suffered here no violence, none oppression, no respect of persons in justice, but *jus equabile*, used to all indifferently.

The 1576 Subsidy Act itself opened in a blaze of self-conscious English specialness:

> The view of the long and present miseries in other realms so nigh us on every side ... causeth us your Majesty's humble subjects to enter into due consideration of the great bliss and happiness which God hath and doth daily pour upon us... [52]

Peace, Protestantism and protection were to be the regime's achievements. They were the goals which all could respect and sympathise with to the extent of parting with money, though the 1571 Subsidy Act had said – all too truthfully for Elizabeth, perhaps – that the subsidy grant was only 'one little and small present'.[53] When by the mid-1580s England was clearly no longer at peace with all her neighbours, the message, though modified, remained essentially the same. There had been, said the act of 1586–87, an *inward* peace 'longer continued than ever before', though Mildmay had said earlier, in 1581, that the Catholics had tried to disrupt it, threatening the very existence of the 'mild Church of the gospel', which he compared favourably with the 'Pope's persecuting Church'.[54] By 1598 the message was a specific reflection of what had been commented on from the start. Taxation had been an investment in the benefits of Elizabeth's reign which had been peace, clemency and justice, and these bounties were to be valued by comparison with the danger facing the country from the yoke of foreign servitude. The final Subsidy Act of the reign in 1601 proclaimed a unity between Queen and subject. It spoke of a practical sympathy with the Queen because she had used taxes to advance the true glory of God and the defence of the 'liberty and felicity of the imperial Crown'.[55] Though taxation was often requested to finance war in Elizabeth's reign, Members of Parliament consciously committed themselves to investing in peace within their own country, which allowed them to enjoy a native clemency and justice from a Queen who had not made the cardinal errors of her half-sister. In the post-Armada parliament of 1589 Sir Christopher Hatton started the subsidy business in the Commons in what has been described as probably one of the best speeches ever delivered in the House. Its potency depened in no small part on its capturing the essence of what we have been exploring: 'We are bound to defend ourselves, our wives, our children, our friends; it is by an instinct of nature. We are bound to defend our country, our prince, our state, our laws,our liberties; ... we are bound to defend our possessions, our liberties, our goods and our lands: it wholly concerneth our profit.'[56]

The topic of parliamentary taxation provides an illuminating insight into the mentality of the gentlemen of England. There was no doubt that it was necessary to protect England from the ravages of its foes. Yet there seems to have been a belief that levying subsidies should not be too much of a financial strain for the wealthier subjects of the land. Elizabeth's own contribution was immense, and a greater number of poorer subjects had been recruited to the ranks of taxpayers by the later part of the reign. Multiple subsidy grants had been accepted as unavoidable by then, but to an extent they were a symbolic testimony to the willingness of the governing classes to assist their monarch, because they were not a reflection of true wealth, and the yields were not enough to meet the Queen's bills. Perhaps this is a sign of weakening cohesion between crown and governors since the Henrician days.[57]

It is, though, just as likely that the English Parliament simply did not see the necessity for greater generosity as long as Spain could not apparently mount a really effective threat in any case. Every time a new round of taxation was requested the cry was, after all, that Protestant England had already survived malicious threats, and it was clear that the last subsidy – inadequate and poorly collected as it was – had served its immediate purpose. Surviving one crisis at a time seemed to be the order of the day. As the Queen, for her own temperamental reasons as well as those dictated by the limitations of finance, conducted a limited rather than an adventurous foreign policy, there was probably never any compelling reason to abandon the peculiarly English penchant for just making do. What we have been considering was, in effect, a system of parliamentary taxation which endorsed the patriotic needs of the monarchy and the realm, but which left effective control of their wealth with the gentlemen governors. The political wisdom of explaining the need for money was recognised from the start, and underlying this a consensus about the nature of the needs ensured that all patriots could endorse the demands. The trouble in 1586–87 over the suggestion that an additional amount of money be given the Queen shows this to perfection. Here patriotism was manifested in a precise form, though far too precise for the Queen herself. There was the curious spectacle of the Queen apparently on the verge of turning down additional grants simply because she would be bound to a particular line of action. This was only one area in which Elizabeth found that Parliament could produce pressure for a distinct line of policy with which she could not agree.

NOTES

1 Lehmberg, *Later Parliaments of Henry VIII*, pp. 271–3; Graves, *Tudor Parliaments*, pp. 80–2; Schofield, 'Taxation and the political limits of the Tudor state'; Alsop, 'Theory and practice of Tudor taxation'; Guy, *Tudor England*, pp. 192, 381; *PE*, pp. 154–5.

2 *PE*, pp. 153–4.

3 Heal, 'Clerical tax collection under the Tudors', pp. 113–22; Guy, *Tudor England*, pp. 381, 383; Elton, *Tudor Constitution*, p. 41.

4 *Procs.*, pp. 33–9.

5 *PE*, p. 158; Alsop, 'Parliament and taxation', pp. 95, 96, and n. 14.

6 *Procs.*, p. 37; *SR*, iv.384, 638; MacCaffrey, 'Parliament and foreign policy', p. 78.

7 *EP*, ii.205, 413.

8 *EP*, i.124; *SR*, iv.465.

9 Alsop, 'Parliament and taxation', especially pp. 91–2.

10 E.g. *EP*, i.348–9, ii.207; cf. *PE*, 158–9.

11 Alsop, 'Parliament and taxation', p. 101.

12 *Procs.*, pp. 528, 541; *EP*, ii.54–7, 411–16.

13 BL Harley MS 283, fo. 35 cited in *PE*, pp. 156–7, and n.18.

14 D'Ewes, *Journals*, p. 632: Wingfield's concern about legislation 'seeing the subsidy was granted'.

15 Alsop, 'Parliament and taxation', p. 97.

16 See Schofield, 'Taxation and the political limits of the Tudor state', p. 228 and n.; *PE*, pp. 156–7.

17 *CJ*, i.74; *EP*, i.137, 139.

18 *Procs.*, pp. 129–39.

19 *PE*, pp. 366, 371, though attributing the speech to Lambarde; Alsop, 'Parliament and Taxation', p. 99.

20 *Procs.*, pp. 141–4.

21 Alsop, 'Reinterpreting the Elizabethan Commons'; *EP*, i.136–9, 141, 143, 168–9.

22 New York Library, Pierpont Morgan MS MA 276, pp. 28–51, especially p. 40.

23 *EP*, ii.181–3; BL Harley MS 7188, especially fos. 100v–2; D'Ewes, *Journals*, p. 414.

24 *EP*, ii.166–83.

25 Alsop, 'Parliament and taxation', p. 97; *EP*, ii.384, 411–16; BL Stowe MS 362, fo. 67.

26 *EP*, ii.55.

27 *EP*, ii.359; BL Stowe MS 362, fo. 68.

28 See below, p. 51, this chapter.

29 *SR*, iv.388, 469; HMC, *Salisbury*, iii.429 for the expectation that this would increase yields; *EP*, i.125; *PE*, p. 161 (though 'commissioners' should be 'assessors', p. 165).

30 *SR*, iv.505–19; Alsop, 'Reinterpreting the Elizabethan Commons', pp. 219, 229.

31 *EP*, i.125.

32 *APC* 1588–89, pp. 413–14.

33 Guy, *Tudor England*, pp. 381–4; D'Ewes, *Journals*, pp. 359, 483; Alsop, 'Parliament and taxation', p. 93, n.6; Williams, *Tudor Regime*, p. 71.

34 See, e.g., *Procs.*, pp. 85, 186.

35 *EP*, i.122; *SR*, iv.282–3: 2 & 3 Ph. and Mary, c.6 (1555).

36 *EP*, i.122.

37 *Procs.*, pp. 202–3, 245; *PE*, pp. 101–2; *EP*, i.218–20.

38 BL Cotton MS Titus Fii, fos. 35v, 48v–9; Russell, 'English parliaments', p. 198; *EP*, ii.300, 308.

39 D'Ewes, *Journals*, pp. 440–1, 442–4, 446, 448; Croft, 'Parliament, purveyance and the city of London'.

40 D'Ewes, *Journals*, pp. 632–3.

41 BL Lansdowne MS 55, fos. 180–3v, 186v–7; Neale (*EP*, ii.206–7) considered this speaker to be Henry Jackman.

42 *EP*, ii.307–9.

43 D'Ewes, *Journals*, p. 458; Schofield, 'Taxation and the political limits of the Tudor state', p. 239.

44 BL Cotton MS Titus Fii, fo. 53v; *EP*, ii.302, 311.

45 *Procs.*, p. 506; *EP*, ii.55.

46 BL Cotton MS Titus Fii, fo. 50.

47 *PE*, pp. 166–7 (for 1571), and cf. pp. 155, 159, 160.

48 *PE*, p. 168; Alsop, 'Parliament and taxation', p. 100; *Procs.*, p. 38.

49 E.g. *PE*, pp. 154–5 and Guy, *Tudor England*, pp. 381–2.

50 *Procs.*, p. 184.

51 Cf. Fussner (ed.), 'William Camden's "Discourse"', p. 206.

52 *Procs.*, pp. 36, 184–5, 442; *SR*, iv.384, 639.

53 *SR*, iv.568.

54 *SR*, iv.778; *Procs.*, pp. 502–4.

55 *SR*, iv.937–8, 991–2.

56 *EP*, ii.195, 200–1.

57 Schofield, 'Taxation and the political limits of the Tudor state', p. 255.

Chapter 4

State matters

Although Members of Parliament had concerns of their own to pursue at Westminster, much time was devoted to the task of safeguarding the dynasty. This was part of the general command to members of both Lords and Commons which was outlined in their writs of summons, namely that they should consult for the protection of the Queen and the realm. Much of the political character of Elizabeth's regime was drawn from an awareness of its existence in a potentially hostile Catholic Europe, and of its arrival on the scene, almost providentially, after the Catholic pro-Spanish interval of Mary Tudor's reign. Elizabeth's own agenda was apparent in Bacon's words in 1559, and has already been referred to.[1] He drew attention at the start of the session to 'the state and condition of the realm and the losses and decays that have of late happened to the imperial crown thereof'. This would be reformed by

> a princess, I say, that is not ... so wedded to her own will and fantasy, that for the satisfaction thereof, she will do anything that were likely to bring any bondage or servitude to her people, or give any just occasion to them of any inward grudge whereby any tumults or stirs might arise, as hath done of late days, ... a princess that never meaneth nor intendeth ... for any private affection to advance the cause or quarrel of any foreign power or potentate to the destruction of her subjects, to the loss of any of her dominions.

Though Mary was not mentioned by name, the intended comparison was clear. Recent history thus provided a yardstick, and the Catholicism of Mary Tudor, and indeed of Mary Stuart, could only be defeated by a Protestantism which could survive short-term threats and promise long-term hopes for posterity.[2]

Elizabeth's parliaments

In a way, the past was against Elizabeth. During the 1530s and 1540s her father had protected himself from his enemies at home by passing new treason laws, and his matrimonial shifts had required parliamentary redefinitions of the order of succession. Henry's Succession Act of 1544 (together with his will) threw her personal solitude into sharp focus, for she was the last person named in it. It was not surprising that men could readily agree on the need to protect the Queen from the most obvious sources of danger in an increasingly hostile world. Parliament would grant taxation, and action could be taken against Catholic dissidents at home: a safe Elizabeth was a safe England. Under these circumstances the legislative response of the Elizabethan state was natural, even predictable and necessary. In 1570, the papal bull *Regnans in excelsis* sought to provide a justification for Elizabeth's deposition by Catholics, and excommunicated her. The following year an act was passed to outlaw such pronouncements. Ten years later came the act to 'retain the Queen's Majesty's subjects in their due obedience', making it treason to convert subjects to Roman Catholicism with the intention of destroying their natural obedience to the Queen, and in 1585 the act against Jesuits and seminary priests provided drastic penalties against 'disturbers of the peace of the realm' who were aiming at Elizabeth's destruction.[3]

ELIZABETH AND THE SUCCESSION

The question of who should succeed to the English throne after Elizabeth preoccupied political circles in England from the moment she came to the throne. She might have solved the problem by marrying and providing issue of her own, or failing this, she could have nominated an heir. As we know, advancing years gradually ruled out the former of these solutions, and she refused to name her successor. This caused desperate anxiety in her subjects, though it was arguably diminished after the execution of Mary Stuart in 1587. In the event the Tudor dynasty served out its time peacefully, but in the process men had been driven to a state of chronic and despairing frustration by Elizabeth's unwillingness to follow her father's example and determine the matter by parliamentary statute. She believed, it is often assumed, that to do so would invite the very disorder and factional dispute that others thought inactivity itself would produce. As her refusal to marry, or clear up the matter of the succession, continued, however, the dangers from Mary Stuart increased. The Scottish queen had laid claim to Elizabeth's throne in 1559, and as the reign progressed she grew more menacing.

The problem was urgent at the outset because of the nature of Henry Vlll's Succession Act of 1544. Should Elizabeth die without an obvious heir, there was a case for arguing that Henry's elder sister Margaret's line had prior claim. This would mean that Mary stood to benefit. Yet it was inconceivable to many that this Catholic queen of Scotland – who had refused to recognise Elizabeth's right to the English throne – should be countenanced. The memory of Mary Tudor's regime, with its foreign influences, if not its Catholicism, was too strong to allow contemplation of a Scot, especially with Mary's strong French connections. The best answer was to persuade Elizabeth to marry and produce children so that the prescribed order of succession could be naturally perpetuated. For a while, then, there was pressure on Elizabeth to marry, evident in the first parliament of the reign in a Commons petition presented by the Speaker and the Privy Councillors in the House urging Elizabeth to marry. Apparently, as she said, this contained no limitation of place or person, despite a rumour that voices had been raised in favour of an English husband.[4] By the 1560s, however, attention was also paid to the connected, though different aim of persuading the Queen to name a successor. In the light of her severe smallpox attack in 1562, it is understandable that this should appear on Parliament's list of desiderata, though the request to marry was also reiterated.[5]

Elizabeth welcomed pressure on neither count, though she continued to get it on both.[6] Given the basic concerns for England and its safety which concerned men in Council and Parliament, it is unlikely that this pressure was confined to a small group of men distinguished by a zealous Protestantism. Political stability was a basic requirement for all, including most of the Catholics, who would not welcome political disruptions, even for the sake of advancing the cause of a Catholic monarch. The succession issue had been high on the political agenda in England since the early 1530s in one way or another, reason enough in itself for all to want to see the options narrowed now. It is true that there was no apparent unity among Elizabeth's leading men as to who should succeed if Elizabeth did not marry. However, all wanted the Queen to do something to solve the problem and were prepared to exert pressure in Commons and

Lords. Their divisions may be less important than their overriding unity of purpose, and they called on her to make the choice. In this light it is unnecessary to look too hard for evidence of campaigns and concerted action in the Commons. It is probably impossible to locate conclusively: the issue was big enough and live enough to generate its own momentum.[7]

The notion of an independent pressure group, the 'choir', has been replaced recently by the suggestion that some members initiated debate in the Commons on instruction from William Cecil, as anxious as anyone to see an end to the uncertainty. It has been argued that Dean Nowell preached the famous pre-session sermon to the members in 1563 on instruction from Robert Dudley. In it he bewailed the disastrous consequences of an unsettled succession. Signs of really orchestrated activity are evident later on, in the 1566 session. One member of the Commons, John Molyneux, who was once thought to be part of the mythical 'Puritan choir', was instructed by William Cecil to raise the matter of the succession, and later on William Lambarde, another client of Cecil's, brought up the question of the subsidy grant in conjunction with the succession. These links are speculative, however, and the truth about who was working with whom at this time may never be fully established. Whether he was acting as a spokesman, or merely expressing his own concerns, there can be little reason to doubt that Molyneux wanted action on marriage and succession. He may have thought that getting the subsidy started would be an inducement to Elizabeth to press on with this business. He may, instead, have wanted to withhold the grant if she did not. It was juxtaposing subsidy and succession which probably mattered, and Elizabeth was hardly more likely to respond to a 'carrot' than was she to a 'stick' which threatened financial deprivation.[8]

The notion that a co-ordinated minority group provided the pressure on Elizabeth at this point is open to serious doubt. There was undoubtedly widespread and intense support for the solution of this problem, so that campaigning, whether from officially inspired quarters or from unofficial rebellious elements, was scarcely necessary, at least to ensure that the matter was raised. It still looks as though we have to contemplate the possibility that the Commons were for a time 'out of control' (one of Neale's favourite phrases). This was because it can hardly have suited Cecil's purposes for the Commons to run ahead too fast, as arguably it did when it gave wide suppport to

Lambarde's call for a settlement of the succession. The Secretary's own preferred target may have been to persuade the Queen to marry. Although he may have been willing to use parliamentary pressure to extract some decision from Elizabeth, some Privy Councillors like Sadler felt that this was not the way to get the Queen's co-operation. He thought she should be left alone to solve the problem.[9] Any disagreements about the best way to proceed naturally became irrelevant when Elizabeth intervened. She had said in 1563 that she was prepared to marry, and parliamentary involvement was unnecessary. Cecil himself was one of three Councillors apparently instructed to tell the Commons to end discussion of the matter.[10]

This produced real conflict with the Queen, and a good deal of uneasy confusion in the Commons about what could safely be said about matters like this. A Commons committee drafted a document which asserted that the Queen's command to stop talking about the succession infringed the House's 'lawful liberties', a claim which prompted Elizabeth to deny that there had been any displeasure towards members, or 'any other thing that might prejudice them'. Their liberties, she said, were not in danger. While the Commons may have been reassured about this aspect of the quarrel, it remained the case that nothing had been done about marriage, or succession, the issues which had provoked it. It may be understandable therefore that the issues were not raised again in the same way. By the end of this session it was probably clear to all that petitions about the succession would never make headway with Elizabeth. From now on, concern about the succession was more narrowly focused. It was aimed specifically at removing the Stuart claim to the throne, a policy which must at first have seemed more likely to succeed in the light of Mary's activity against Elizabeth. If the Queen could not be persuaded to say who would succeed her, surely she would agree to disqualify someone who had claimed the English throne.[11]

THE QUEEN'S SAFETY AND MARY STUART

The instruction given to both Houses by the Lord Keeper in 1571 that they should 'do well to meddle with no matters of state but such as should be propounded unto them' was not encouraging. Parliament was called in the aftermath of the Northern Rising of 1569, partly to consider a new treason law. Elizabeth was not, however, prepared to allow this new legislation to be extended so as to exclude her Scottish cousin from the succession. This was the purpose of one of Thomas Norton's proposed changes to the bill, and he tried to achieve it by means of an additional clause. This declared that the aiders and abettors of anyone claiming a title to the Crown should be guilty of treason, but its wide-ranging scope with regard to the claimants themselves needs to be stressed. It proposed that 'whosoever in her [Elizabeth's] life hath done, or shall make claim to the imperial Crown of this realm, that he, or they, or their heirs, to be forbarred of any claim, challenge or title to be made to the Crown at any time hereafter'.[12]

Whether or not Norton's work in this instance was specifically commissioned by Councillors, it soon became widely supported in both houses. If passed, the remodelled Treasons Bill would have immediately excluded Mary and her son James, born in 1566, from the English succession. Mary's past activities would have condemned her, and James would have suffered simply by virtue of being her son. In the end, Norton's far-reaching changes did not see the light of day, and it is reasonable to suppose that this resulted from Elizabeth's predictable hostility to it. The Lords and Commons probably had no choice, even without the Queen's prompting, but to dilute Norton's propositions. To stand firm on them would only have jeopardised the whole measure, which in itself still offered the prospect of catching Mary if she actively worked against the Crown. This practical consid-eration casts doubt on the view that the episode was of minor impor-tance in the quest for settlement of the succession. Norton's move was a bold one, and it was well supported in the first place. It cannot be true to say that the succession issue encountered 'general silence' in 1571, though no one apparently called on the Queen to settle the matter. There was clearly some retreat from what Norton and others wanted, but this arose as much from an awareness that the Com-mons had an enormous political capacity to influence the Queen to react in a *negative* way, and may therefore be seen as a strategic withdrawal.[13]

By this stage two cardinal principles of Elizabeth's thought had become apparent. There should be no retrospective scope to the act, and Mary was not to suffer for deeds declared illegal only after the event. Secondly, the act was not to involve the heirs of claimants, simply by virtue of their being heirs. As passed, the act of 1571 affirmed that it was treasonable to plan to kill or harm the Queen.

Anyone claiming title in future was to be disabled from inheriting the throne. It also became treason for anyone to affirm a title to the throne for any claimant disabled by virtue of any proclamation issued according to the act.[14] In the end, Mary lost her life, and therefore her own claim to the throne, because she offended the act of 1585 by becoming involved in the Babington plot.

Norton's contribution to the measure in 1571 had dramatically transformed it into an exclusion bill. This is hardly surprising coming after the events of the 1560s, though it has to be stressed: Mary was not wanted, and neither was her son. This was not the wish of a Puritan, or any other small, rebellious clique, but a political position shared by many in Elizabeth's parliaments. This anti-Scottish feeling occupied a central position in the thinking of many of Elizabeth's governors. The point is graphically made by a speech drafted by Sir Ralph Sadler, probably for the session of 1563 or 1566.[15] When the Commons petitioned Elizabeth in 1563 to marry and settle the succession they showed clearly enough that they were aware of, and opposed to the dangers and possibilities of a foreign assumption of the Crown. In Sadler's own case, the feeling in some legal circles that the law made it impossible for Mary Stuart to succeed to the English throne was reinforced by his steadfast opposition as 'a mere natural Englishman' to being 'subject to a foreign prince of a strange nation'. He regarded any inclination to allow Mary a title as 'unnatural'. The significance of a Privy Councillor's commitment to this view cannot be underestimated. Arguably, there was no one better to present this case than Sadler. His long first-hand experience of the Scots, since Henry VIII's reign when he had tried to negotiate the marriage of the Prince Edward to the then Princess Mary, had shaped his mind. At that time he had apparently favoured the view that union between England and Scotland would be beneficial to both. Yet the Scottish view that nationalist feeling and, more pertinently perhaps, popular hostility would cry out against it weighed heavily with him in the end, he said. He concluded his speech with what can only be seen as a veiled threat that any agreement that Mary should succeed would mean that 'our common people and the stones in the street would rebel against it'.[16]

Anti-Stuart feeling obviously persisted, as was soon apparent in the next session of 1572 called to deal with the exceptionally dangerous circumstances of the Ridolphi Plot on Elizabeth's life and Mary's involvement in it. Presumably, the sheer pressure of events forced Elizabeth to consult Parliament about the possibility of new laws for her safety. This was the only occasion on which taxation was not requested, and it looks as though she was not happy at the prospect of having to react to Mary's complicity in the plot. She may have hoped, however, that divisions would develop in Council and Parliament, and that she would not need to take action against Mary.[17]

On 13 May the Queen's legal officers none the less told members of both Houses that since Elizabeth'a accession Mary had offended on many counts, including laying claim to the throne. Elizabeth no doubt wanted discussion to concentrate on providing against further attempts on her life, for Bacon's opening speech stressed that Parliament's purpose was the Queen's safety.[18] If so, she was disappointed, because a Kentish member, Thomas Scott, was only one of many who believed that the unsettled succession needed to be addressed as well, and that Mary's ability to be a nuisance would last as long as the issue remained open. 'The Queen's Majesty hath now tarried so long', he said, 'she can tarry no longer. It remaineth only, if she do, her nobility to be spoiled, her realm conquered, and herself deposed.'[19] It was clear to all that Mary had committed high treason, but not clear whether Elizabeth would punish her. In the end, neither of the two bills drawn up by a joint committee of the Houses proved to be palatable to Elizabeth. On the one hand, she could accept the fact of Mary's crime and the penalty of death, together with a declaration against her claim to succeed. On the other, Mary would stand debarred from the succession, though untouched for deeds already committed. Though this latter, milder measure was drafted so as to leave Mary's heir untouched as long as he was not party to future plots, it is easy to understand that Elizabeth had no option but to reject it, as she did the other bill. Indeed, it remained true that the less severe bill, if passed, would have provided a basis for Mary's death in the event of *future* activities against Elizabeth, including claiming the title. An amendment also underlined the determination of men in Parliament that Mary 'shall not at any time have, hold, claim, possess or enjoy' the Crown.[20] Since Mary's activities seemed to be based on a claim to the throne, it is hard to see how Elizabeth could accede to a measure which would constitute a victory for Councillors, Commons and Lords in their quest for exclusion. The debates over the redrafting of the milder bill could not have made the Commons' hostility clearer, since members were determined to avoid any implication that by positively barring Mary from the succession they had tacitly accepted the legitimacy of her claim – or indeed that of her son – in the first place. A proviso was added which declared that nothing in the bill was to be taken to imply any allowance of a claim to the succession to *any* person or persons whatsoever.[21]

Disappointment over this episode in 1572 was immense. As we shall see, it played a large role in Peter Wentworth's intervention in 1576. The 1571 Treason Act had failed as a deterrent and Mary's continued willingness to engage in plots meant that Elizabeth was still in danger. In the turmoil which might follow Elizabeth's death a leisurely and ordered implementation of the law would be impossible in any case. It is hardly surprising therefore that news of Throckmorton's plot convinced the Privy Council in 1584 that something had to be done immediately to provide for future dangers. For all the understandable desperation of its signatories, the infamous Bond of Association which emerged remains chillingly brutal. Hundreds of respectable gentlemen of England bound themselves by solemn sealed oath to hunt down to the death anyone who attempted to kill Elizabeth, together with their heirs. Despite Elizabeth's known antipathy to taking action against James unless he himself became involved against her, the governors of England pledged themselves to his death in the event of a plot conducted on his, and his mother's behalf. Not being party to the plot would save neither him, nor his mother. The Bond may have been a stopgap measure pending a new parliament and a new law. In the proceedings which followed, however, Elizabeth remained firm. Predictably, she insisted that any new law should be a safety measure rather than a pretext for excluding candidates to the throne without due cause.[22]

A new act emerged in 1585 after an initial bill had been rejected. The intention of the new act was both to deter plots, and to avoid the dreadful outcome of a successful one. It differed from the 1571 Treason Act in important respects. The earlier act prescribed action at common law. Now, in 1585, Elizabeth's subjects would be allowed, at her direction, to hunt down those who were judged of involvement in conspiracy by a state commission of enquiry. These might be claimants to the throne, or those aiding and abetting them. Any claimants involved were to be disabled from inheriting the Crown, a device, presumably, designed to weaken them in the event of delays in their apprehension. This had been a feature of the first bill, though it had also included the heirs of claimants at this point. If the Queen were killed, those for whom and by whom the deed was carried out should be excluded from any title, as well as their issue 'being any wise assenting or privy to the same'. The act did not specify that the *claimant's* knowledge of, or consent to the plot were necessary to debar from the title. It may be that this was an attempt to deal with a potential situation where a claimant might assert innocence of any plot to kill the monarch, while still trying to hold a claim to the title intact. Furthermore, anyone obstructing the implementation of the act would lose any claim they might have to the throne themselves. The scope of the act was thus more narrowly drawn than the first bill which had addressed its attention to plots against the Queen's life – successful or not – undertaken to advance a claimant to the throne. In that event both claimant and heirs were to be excluded from any title, whether party or not to the plots.[23]

The act thus left James's claim untouched if he remained innocent of plots and killings. Both the Bond and the first bill had disabled him, whether or not he were party to any plot against the Queen's title. It may therefore be accounted a 'victory' for the Queen over her advisers in Council and Parliament. On the other hand, there was the possibility that Mary might be excluded in the event of Elizabeth's death, though not party to the action. This was perhaps a bonus for those who by this time could consider the Protestant James to be a potential successor to the English throne. Elizabeth had also agreed that in the event of her death a state commission, about a third of whom were to be drawn from 'lords of the Parliament not being of the Privy Council', could decide whether claimants and their heirs were guilty.[24] In this way she had contemplated a situation, albeit beyond her life, where her subjects would have in effect a statutory power to exclude from the exclusion. The act of 1585 also had to deal with the fact that Elizabeth's leading subjects were not only bound by the Bond, but also by the act itself, and that the two were incompatible. This was achieved, albeit awkwardly, by a reinterpretation of what the Bond had said in the first place. While the Bond required action against persons 'pretending title', this was now to be interpreted strictly according to the act of Parliament and 'not against any other person or persons'. This was the statutory acknowledgement that the battle in Parliament for the Stuart exclusion was over. James could become King if he behaved himself.[25]

For many years there had thus been considerable disagreement between the Queen and her leading subjects. Elizabeth had been at odds with her Councillors, Commons, and Lords for many years about how best to secure her safety and that of the realm. Perhaps this was inevitable since potential successors to the throne were involved, let alone a rival claimant. The positive outcome had been slow to emerge and limited in scope. Though the act of 1585 was a product of co-operation between the Houses and the Queen, it frustrated the larger hopes of many. These disagreements are important, moreover, because they were expressed in a way which, if anything, reinforced the divide between Queen and subject. While the viewpoints in the 'row' are clear enough, the reasoning employed by the participants reveal assumptions about government and princely duties on the one hand, and the tactical limitations of some of Elizabeth's responses on the other.

Elizabeth's reaction to the early pressure was to resort to enigmatism, thanking her subjects in Parliament for their concern and requests that she marry, but at the same time promising nothing. She was, however, arguably unwise to give the clear impression that she would consider marriage. She said famously in 1559 that she was not inclined to marry at the moment, though she could change her mind. She said that 'whensoever it may please God to incline my heart to another kind of life', her people could rest assured she would choose her husband wisely. She also offered an additional promise of security, saying that if it became apparent that God wished her to remain single then she would nominate an heir 'in convenient time' to be a 'fit governor and peradventure more beneficial to the realm than such offspring as may come of me'. Her general approval of the petition – because it did not try to limit her to 'place or person' – fell far short of a ban on raising the issue subsequently. When it duly re-emerged in 1563, she again left herself open to justifiable pressure by saying of the Commons' petition that 'of the matter and sum thereof I like and allow very well'. More to the point, perhaps, the Queen had promised that if she did not marry she would none the less settle the succession, though everyone naturally assumed that this would be done publicly, and not remain locked in Elizabeth's mind.[26]

The solidarity of the Commons and Lords became evident in 1563, prompted in part by the Queen's illness shortly before the session. By 1 February both Houses had produced petitions which expressed their fears of Catholicism and disorder, and their concern for the preservation of England, both for the present and for posterity. The Commons justified their action on the basis of the Lord Keeper's opening address, which they said directed them to this matter by calling for the establishment and enhancement of the safety of the realm. This instruction seemed to signify, they said, that Elizabeth had indeed called Parliament for the settlement of 'matters of greatest weight', because achieving 'some certain limitation to guide the obedience of posterity' was unsurpassed in importance. Though Elizabeth would not concede that Parliament had a claim to this sort of discussion, it is easy to see how men in both Houses found it impossible to see that anything else they might do could endure unless this basic need were met. Though the Lords merely claimed it would be *convenient* to settle the matter now that Parliament was in being, they did attempt to pressurise the Queen by insisting that she had a duty to God to resolve it. They had discharged their own duty by raising the subject. Commons and Lords emphasised the practical consideration which concerned all men of government of whatever station, namely that in the event of Elizabeth's death there would be no known source of power from which all authority in the land must derive. All the day-to-day running of the regime would be in suspense and lack validity. This was itself a situation which would-be claimants to the throne could use to their advantage: 'the realm may thereby become a prey to strangers'. The Queen was obviously angered by this general assault on her position, and her response to the Commons was almost instinctive, and arguably crude. There was a promise to answer soon – which was not kept – and a reminder of her queenly position. Resorting to rank was not perhaps surprising in itself. What is significant is the political and social pre-eminence of those against whom this weapon was so frequently unleashed. Taking up the point that the lives of her subjects were in danger from uncertainty about the succession, she riposted that *they* would merely lose their lives, whereas *she* would have to answer to God if she made the wrong decision. Her mortal soul was in danger. She treated her Commons to a painful demonstration of her supreme authority: 'I trust you ... do not forget that by me you were delivered whilst you were hanging on the bough ready to fall into the mud, yea to be drowned in the dung.' None of the substance of this was new, naturally, though what was needed was a real answer.[27]

Members of both Houses may have drawn some comfort from Elizabeth's speech, delivered by Bacon at the end of the session, which appeared to offer some hope for progress in this matter. While she said nothing about her marriage – because, with a curious logic, she said this was unnecessary since everyone hoped that a child of hers would succeed – the speech was apparently amended to imply that she would marry. She also hoped she would be able to die 'in quiet with *nunc dimittis*', knowing that her subjects' security had been assured, presumably an answer to the Lords' point that she needed to heed her responsibility to God. It is difficult to see how the point can have escaped the Queen that her subjects wanted to preserve the benefits of her rule, benefits which derived much of their force from an acute awareness of Mary Tudor's shortcomings. Yet in the years after 1563 the issue became more intense because of the continued refusal to treat the matter as anything but private and personal to her. Though men of government appealed to her sense of public duty as a queen who loved her subjects, their requests fell on ears stubbornly closed to arguments from political considerations about good order and the necessity to avoid chaos and anarchy.[28]

When she was asked in 1566 to fulfil the 'promise' to marry which she had given in 1563, Elizabeth responded, once again with little more than side-stepping ploys. A decision to see a delegation from both Houses pre-empted the presentation of a petition, though the activity and the anxiety which underpinned it could not be denied, and she was again forced into endorsing her promise to marry. As far as the settlement of succession was concerned, it was not convenient 'at this present'. Her subsequent demands to stop further discussion of the matter produced the constitutional difficulties we have already seen. It also signalled the emergence of the Wentworth brothers into Elizabethan parliamentary history, because Paul was moved to frame three questions. Had these been answered, they might have helped to determine who was properly able to instruct the House to cease debate. The truth was that the deep commitment to Elizabethan rule, which her loyal subjects in Lords and Commons wanted to preserve, meant that there was no option but to suffer Elizabeth's refusal to settle the succession. This was perhaps a godsend to her own temperament and political style, but it could not disguise the fact that she was in dispute with the leading men in her government. Here was a continuing difference of attitude, and it highlighted the fact that she conducted personal monarchy on distinctly personal lines. Her ministers longed for more 'public' concern from Elizabeth, but they looked in vain. If a surviving draft of her speech may be believed, she was even prepared to tell Parliament in 1566 that it would have been better if she had initiated the matter of succession, not members of the Houses.[29]

It is easy to see how the Northern Rising and the Ridolfi Plot added to the anxieties of members, even before the events of the 1572 session which sorely tried their patience further. The argument which many members then relied on, namely that Mary Queen of Scots was liable to the penalties of treason in England, drew much of its substance from thought which justified resistance to monarchs, and which had been adopted by the exiles in Mary Tudor's reign. To this extent, resistance theory became 'another coin in the political currency of England', and it must have provided another reason, if she needed one, for Elizabeth to resist the pressure being exerted on her in this direction.[30] Even though the argument was being deployed in this case against a monarch who was herself treacherously resisting Elizabeth, the latter can hardly have been happy to give public endorsement to it by assenting to either of the measures proposed in Parliament.[31]

There was another aspect of this parliamentary thought which was more audacious because of the directness of its attack on Elizabeth herself. It could, on its own, have ensured that the Commons were sent away from this session empty-handed on this issue. A paper prepared by Thomas Dannet, member for Maidstone in Kent, and a man by no means obscure and distant from prominent courtiers, said that Elizabeth should do her utmost to protect her subjects' safety by prolonging her own life, even if she refused to heed it after her death by nominating a successor. If she failed to do so, her subjects, 'despairing of safety by her means shall be forced to seek protection elsewhere, to the end they be not altogether destitute of defence'.[32] It is by no means clear what this could mean. Perhaps it was a threat. Its vagueness could indicate that Englishmen would turn to another monarch, a staggering suggestion, not least in its naivety, for Elizabeth can hardly have been persuaded that her subjects would willingly espouse rebellion in order to replace her on the throne, even if it were possible for all to agree on a suitable alternative. The assertion looks suspiciously like whistling in the dark, and Elizabeth must have known it. As the session wore on and it became apparent that there would be no real progress, some members had been driven into this ridiculous corner by a sense of neglect and danger. Hopes had been boosted at the start of the session; now it looked as though Elizabeth would do nothing yet again. It began to appear that Parliament had been called in vain, and one member at least gave voice to the hope that the session would not 'pass without doing of anything'.[33]

There was, however, an idea which lay behind any resistance thought and which was arguably more significant. It had appeared before, and it was that Elizabeth herself was not discharging her responsibilities to God and her subjects. Given that recent events produced compelling reasons for the Scottish queen's early death, Elizabeth's steadfast determination not to be moved could only be explained now in some quarters in one way. This was that she was simply not aware of the dangers to which her inactivity was exposing her people. The idea did not come from 'rebellious' corners of the Commons; it first appeared from no less a person than the Master of Requests, Thomas Wilson, who said he 'doubteth whether she so fully seeth her own peril' when he spoke on 19 May. In another version of the speech he is recorded as saying that Elizabeth 'desireth to proceed more mildly, not seeing the danger she standeth in'. This was to say in not so many words that the Queen was not capable of taking appropriate or correct political action on this issue, and to argue that Parliament knew better. Against this background it was hardly surprising that the House wanted the stronger of the two bills against the Scottish queen. She must be executed for the high treason she had already committed.[34]

In this the Lords were ready to join the Commons, but when Elizabeth rejected these calls, the Commons again heard the view that their Queen was not sufficiently vigilant. 'Her Majesty be lulled asleep and wrapped in the mantle of her own peril', said one member.[35] Another was of the opinion that 'she hath so small regard unto herself', and Peter Wentworth regretted her rejection of the 'better' bill against Mary in order to 'follow the worse, to the danger of her person, subversion of religion, destruction of the realm and all her good subjects'. Demands that the Commons ask Privy Council members to 'incite and stir her Majesty in this behalf' must have been offensive to her.[36] All this emphasised that, despite undoubted loyalty and commitment to the Protestant Elizabethan state, there was a role for personal criticism of the Queen and her own policy. This has for long been a feature of the older views that Elizabeth's rebellious 'Puritan choir' were men who tried uncomfortably to square the circle of dissident loyalty. What has to be stressed is that the apparently contorted political spirits of the time were to be found in every corner of the establishment itself, driven there by a queen whose answer to her problems were, by her own admission, often 'answerless'.

PARLIAMENT'S ROLE

To realise this does not mean, however, that theories of 'mixed monarchy' were necessarily in the air. Men were compelled to draw the practical conclusion that if Elizabeth refused to do her duty to God, then they would have to try to provide for the worst contingencies, despite the Queen. As we have already seen, by the time the act of 1585 was passed against Mary Stuart it did contain provision for what was in effect a statutory state commission to determine James's ability to ascend the English throne in the event of Elizabeth's untimely death. To this extent Elizabeth had recognised what had driven leading ministers like Burghley to consider practical provision, if not constitutional novelty, in the form of an interregnum body which could ensure a peaceful transmission of monarchic authority. Her near death from natural causes had already meant that in 1563 the problem of authority in the event of the sovereign's death had been made apparent. There was talk of a bill in the Lords which would have allowed Parliamentary authorisation for a proclamation of a new prince.[37]

By 1584 Thomas Digges, the mathematician and scientist member, had produced a scheme for a political stopgap which he hoped would be safeguarded by the creation of an army of 40,000 men to deter invaders. This had been motivated in part by the assertion that the Catholics constantly urged a doctrine of resistance against Elizabeth to justify their attempts on her life. After years of struggle it seemed to many that the situation was still far from satisfactory. Indeed, the Bond of Association itself could be attacked because it was unfair and it would not work. Digges – and there were others, including Wentworth, apparently – thought there was something fundamentally wrong with a situation where an innocent party could be disadvantaged even to the point of being hunted to the death even though not party to the 'hurt' of Elizabeth. Men's consciences were wounded and their minds aggrieved by this, Digges said. What gave rise to desperation was the feeling that the Bond itself could cause instability, even bloodshed. The salve could become very irritating salt. Because there were conscientious doubts about the morality of the Bond, there was no wholesale agreement over how binding it was to be, and if Elizabeth were to be killed, confusion would reign and there would be 'no lawful council of estate' to deal with it. Moreover, doubts about how far the Bond was in conflict with the other oath – the parliamentary oath – which members had sworn 'to her Majesty and the succession' had not been resolved. Digges professed concern therefore that he and others like him could, on the basis of the Bond of Association, be drawn into action against a lawful successor. There *was* such a person, he said, though their identity had not yet been revealed. Tender consciences could not unite behind such an agreement, and in the unthinkable event of Elizabeth's death, the Bond would split the nation by crystallising profound differences among men, thus provoking what it was meant to prevent. Faced with this logic, consciences could do nothing other than resort to an 'interregnum'. Giving it that name, however, inevitably disguises the fact that it had been arrived at by practical and logical considerations, rather than by a philosophical commitment to notions of a new form of government, a kind of regularised 'mixed monarchy'. Digges professed no novelty. He simply asked that the Queen allow her officers to remain in post to sort out problems. Though the request was thus a very practical plea, Elizabeth cannot have failed to see in this a request to divest herself – though dead – of power she had jealously protected since 1559.[38]

Digges may have been involved in Burghley's own efforts at the same time which culminated in a draft bill for the establishment of a Grand Council should Elizabeth be killed. The Council would for the time being be the governing body of the realm, and it would not only seek out and punish the culprits, but would recall the last parliament to have sat before the Queen's death. Though this body, by means of a committee, was to have control of the realm's finances, its main task was to hear all claims to the succession and to determine speedily who had the best claim 'in blood'. It is hard to know what else responsible men of government were to do in view of Elizabeth's dogged refusal to consider any provision for the worst imaginable contingency. They were indeed faced with an unusual situation, though it had been present in varying degrees of intensity for many years. The bill – which never came before the Houses, presumably because of Elizabeth's antipathy to it – was sheer pragmatism, and it cannot really be considered as an attempt to produce a 'constitutional monarchy' in some form. Had the real wishes of its authors been fulfilled in any case the bill would have been unnecessary. The parliament to be summoned by the Grand Council would have been of Elizabeth's making, as last assembled before her death, and not one summoned on its own authority *ab initio*. The new monarch was to have a claim through blood, and the Council and the 'interregnum parliament' would then cease to exist. The stopgap arrangements were to be no more lasting than that, and it would soon be royal business as usual.[39]

It is hard to see why it has been argued that Parliament had no role in the Scottish queen's death, for the act of 1585 we have already discussed provided the basis for her attainder, though Elizabeth tried publicly to minimise her own responsibility for the final deed itself. Some of her servants were humiliated to a degree in the process, especially Secretary Davison; but it is possible to see this as a cosmetic subterfuge.[40] Whether Elizabeth really wanted Mary to die at this point or not, her signing of a warrant in pursuit of the act of Parliament is not in doubt. She had at least started the implementation of the act passed at the behest of Parliament. There could be no hiding her own part in Parliament and its work. As Speakers commonly said at the end of sessions, she was the only person who could give life to bills which had passed both Houses. She had been asked to assent to the bill in 1585 so that she and the realm might live on, even at the cost of Mary's own life.[41]

In the debate in 1586 about what was to be done with Mary following the Babington plot, Job Throckmorton supported the idea of Parliament's omnicompetence in the matter. 'May not one write upon the doors of this House, "*Quid non*"? ... Under the warrant of God's law, what may not this House [do]? I mean the three estates of the land.' The answer provided by this episode was precious little when all its constituent parts worked in the same direction. It is conceivable that the same act, as we have seen, went some way towards conceding a power of determining the succession. The minds of the political nation were in turmoil in 1584–85, and Digges's 'Discourse' revealed that more clearly, perhaps, than has hitherto been recognised. After Mary's execution in 1587 all eyes were on James of Scotland. Throckmorton himself said as much when he recognised that all men could now do realistically was to have the pious hope that James, 'a young and wavering head', would not exhibit the failings of his mother.[42]

It may be that men were now content to leave the matter in Elizabeth's hands, that an uneasy realism emerged under the impact of Mary's death and James's adult and kingly, albeit Scottish, Protestantism. It made no sense to go on arguing that Parliament ought to be involved actively in settling the succession. Indeed, now that it suited some Catholics, principally Parsons, to argue that Parliament might vest the succession in a Catholic claimant, men like Wentworth were able to argue that the Queen's power to decide the succesion should be upheld. In fact, no one had ever really said other than that. The Henrician legislation, with which unfavourable comparisons had been made, ratified what the King had already established, or was likely to establish in his own will, and it did so because a number of direct heirs existed in close proximity. What frightened Elizabethans was the unacceptability of the closest candidate, and the confusion which surrounded her. By 1587, the obvious candidate, while by no means perfect, was the best of a very much worse bunch. The goal of preserving a Protestant regime looked much closer to achievement than it had ever been, and the 'parliamentary' aspects of the struggle could be allowed to wither away.[43]

No one expected the Lords and Commons by themselves to be able to enforce a settlement upon Elizabeth. It is not clear, however, that this signifies Parliament's essential unimportance and weakness. Given its role in the constitution, the most it can arguably have done was to demonstrate and articulate the political needs of the nation, and to exert as much pressure as was practical to bring them to fruition. Short of refusing to deal with essential business, or withholding money requested for the defence of the Protestant nation, there was nothing more to be done. In any case, neither of these approaches was guaranteed to elicit a positively favourable response from the Queen. It may never be wholly clear whether Elizabeth's strategy *vis-à-vis* the Houses on this matter was simply to stall and repel in order to guard what she regarded as her own private ground. It is conceivable that she found it useful from time to time to point to the 'excesses' of her subjects in Parliament as a means of influencing and intimidating others, like Mary and James in particular. Whatever the case, the price she paid was arguably high. In this matter there was a divide, if not a gulf, between herself and the broad spectrum of her governors at all levels. The claims that Privy Councillors played an advanced game of strategic manoeuvring in the Commons, and put up members to initiate the matter of marriage and succession, looks doubtful on the current evidence. On the other hand, they were part of a general groundswell of opinion which considered that all practical steps should be taken to deal with the regrettable situation in which their Queen seemed content to leave them. In this sense the 'opposition' which some historians used to see in a small group of outspoken 'rebellious' members needs to be seen as far more significant, because it was in fact far more widespread. Though proceedings in Parliament were not technically public, there could scarcely be any hiding the fact that her ministers, bishops and lords, among others, used Parliament to develop an argument from public duty, while Elizabeth chose to tread a path which she insisted should be her own private domain.

NOTES

1 See Chapter 3, p. 39.

2 *Procs.*, pp. 3–4, 34, 36, 38.

3 *EP*, i.228, 329, 382–9; ii.37.

4 *EP*, i.47; *Procs.*, p. 45.

5 *PE*, pp. 335–8; Elton, *Tudor Constitution*, p. 3; MacCaffrey, *Shaping of the Elizabethan Regime*, especially pp. 112–13, 145–7; *EP*, i.101; Elizabeth's health also caused concern in 1564.

6 See *Procs.*, p. 4.

7 Levine, *Early Elizabethan Succession Question*, pp. 172–3; *PE*, pp. 360–7.

8 See Chapter 3; *Procs.*, pp. 129–39; *PE*, pp. 358, 366–7, 371, 372; Alsop, 'Reinterpreting the Elizabethan Commons'.

9 *Procs.*, pp. 143–4, and see Chapter 3.

10 *EP*, i.152; Elton's account of the succession issue in 1566 is complex and unsatisfactory: it rests on a belief that Cecil wished to concentrate on the Queen's marriage, while others wanted to work at the succession which he knew she would not allow Parliament to become involved in. Even so Molyneux and Lambarde, whom he believes were working for Cecil, both pressed for movement on the succession, a tactic which was risky and likely to antagonise Elizabeth. It also rests on an unsafe assertion that a particular speech which has survived was Lambarde's, and it does not fully account for shifts and changes which arose as the issue unfolded. A large element of speculation is also deployed.

11 *Procs.*, pp. 156–7, 162, 174.

12 *Procs.*, pp. 199, 204; *PE*, p. 183 ignores the prescription for the future in Norton's clause.

13 *PE*, pp. 182–4, 375.

14 *SR*, iv.526–8.

15 *Procs.*, pp. 87–9, 91.

16 *PE*, pp. 182, 184, 359–60; Elton corrects the statement in *Procs.*, p. 55 that Sadler became a councillor only in 1566.

17 *EP*, 241–2; *PE*, p. 185.

18 *Procs.*, p. 317; *EP*, ii.249–51.

19 *Procs.*, pp. 349–50.

20 *Procs.*, p. 307.

21 *EP*, i.253, 257–8, 282, 286–7.

22 *EP*, ii.13–17, 33.

23 *EP*, ii.33, 51–2; *SR*, iv.704–5.

24 See *EP*, ii.52 for this as part of Elizabeth's counter to Burghley's proposals for an interregnum.

25 *EP*, ii.52; *SR*, iv.704–5.

26 *Procs.*, pp. 45, 56, 95.

27 *Procs.*, pp. 58–62, 90, 95.

28 *Procs.*, p. 115.

29 *Procs.*, pp. 145–9, 154, 174.

30 Bowler, '"An axe or an acte"'.

31 Collinson, 'Monarchical republic', p. 408.

32 Bowler, '"An axe or an acte"', p. 353.

33 *Procs.*, pp. 298, 374.

34 *Procs.*, pp. 328, 365; *Commons, sub* Wilson, Thomas.

35 *EP*, i.268, 273, 277.

36 *Procs.*, pp. 373, 382.

37 Collinson, 'Monarchical republic'; *EP*, i.112–13.

38 BL Lansdowne MS 98, fos. 14–18 (Digges's Discourse), especially fos. 14–16; cf. *EP*, ii.44–5.

39 Collinson, 'Monarchical republic', pp. 422–3.

40 *EP*, ii.137–38.

41 *PE*, pp. 376–7.

42 *EP*, ii.111, 172.

43 *EP*, ii.251–66 for Wentworth and the succession issue.

Chapter 5

Parliament
and God's cause

Religious considerations in the broad sense often impinged on the legislative business of Parliament, but it was the question of the nature of the Church itself which became one of the greatest areas of irritation for the Queen.[1] Elizabeth plainly considered that the acts of supremacy and uniformity confirmed her authority as leader of a Church re-liberated from Roman thraldom, yet there has been much debate about how this settlement evolved in the first parliament in 1559. The view that the government wanted merely to establish Elizabeth's supremacy of the Church, and that she was forced by a strong element in the Commons to accept explicit Protestantism all at once, is no longer held, though it was once thought to be eminently sensible. The newer view – that a Protestant settlement beyond the mere re-establishment of her supremacy over the Church was intended from the start – now commands general assent.[2]

THE SETTLEMENT OF 1559 AND ENGLISH SOLIDARITY

As Easter 1559 approached Elizabeth, it seems, could draw no comfort from what had happened in Parliament. The work of the conservative bishops and peers in the Upper House had emasculated the Commons' bill which provided for a Protestant supremacy. If allowed to pass, it would merely have *enabled* her to assume control of the Church, rather than providing a clear statement that she was endowed with it. The decision not to dissolve Parliament, but to recall it after the Easter recess, provided a chance to remedy this deficiency. There was a religious disputation, blatantly rigged against the conservatives, and the arrest of two bishops seems to have been intended to intimidate the bench of Marian bishops generally. When the votes were taken on the revised bills of supremacy and uniformity it was clear that the new order in religion carried no support at all from the Marian bishops, and that there was some positive opposition.[3]

It is easy to see why interpretations of these events have varied so much. Some of the pertinent documentary evidence has not survived, so the nature and origins of bills which are central to the story are uncertain.[4] Neither is the intensity of Elizabeth's own commitment to Protestantism easily established. While her conduct of affairs was unpalatable to orthodox Catholics, she was soon alarming leading newly appointed ecclesiastics with her reluctance to clear her chapel of crucifixes and candles, and by issuing a set of Injunctions which failed to take the more obvious steps towards a *visible* Protestant order in the churches of the land. If the altars of Mary's reign were transformed into Protestant communion tables, it was not Elizabeth who had decreed it at this point, but others going beyond the strict limit of their brief.[5] All this may have been a sign of her own spiritual and religious disposition, but it meant there was a difference, if not a gulf, between her and many around her, both bishops and Councillors. It is this which remains the starting-point for a consideration of the differences between her and her subjects in Parliament.[6]

Elizabeth set great store by the parliamentary settlement, for she had gained an unequivocal statement that she was supreme governor of the Church of England. At the end of the session Bacon stressed that her subjects were bound to obey the laws which had been duly passed after frank discussion. She may have hoped that this would be the end of the matter, but religion became a persistent part of the parliamentary agenda, despite the Queen's wishes. If we refer again to the Lord Keeper's opening address in 1559 it is hard to see how it can have been otherwise. Bacon told the Houses that their task was the 'well making of laws for the according and uniting of the people of this realm into an uniform order of religion to the honour and glory of God, the establishment of his church and tranquility of the realm'. He said that the advancement of God's glory was a firm foundation on which the policy of every good public weal was to be sustained; and he spoke of the need to avoid 'any kind of idolatry or superstition', extremities likely to produce 'fearful punishments and plagues'. The link between religion and stability was clearly stated. It also looks as though Bacon had signalled an anti-Catholic stance whose internal logic could easily demand a removal of 'superstition' from the English Church, if only as a way to greater security at home.[7] Much hinged upon a satisfactory state of religious affairs, therefore, and the line was held throughout the reign. In the final parliament in 1601 the message was reiterated more succinctly when Speaker Croke said 'religion is all in all', and went on to extol the politically binding force of religion as a cement and force for obedience.[8]

Though the Queen did not wish religion to appear on the parliamentary agenda after 1559, the protection of the settlement from Catholic threats at home and abroad was another matter, and new laws were sometimes needed to cope with them. This was a political necessity because it armed the Elizabethan state, and the supremacy, with the legal means to defend itself. It was useful also as a demonstration of national support for the break with Rome of 1559. The debates on these matters resounded with statements about the superior nature of Elizabeth's Church in comparison with the harsh tyranny of Rome. Bacon told the Houses to deal carefully with 'God's cause' in 1563, and to remember that 'cold, lukewarm, doubtful or double-dealing therein cannot but breed ... factions, divisions, dissensions, seditions'. In their petition to Elizabeth about the succession the Commons said everyone should be wary of a 'faction of heretics in your realm, contentious and malicious papists, lest they most unnaturally against their country, most madly against their own safety, and most traiterously against your Highness ... hope of the woeful day of your death'.[9] Any rational appeal to the argument that English Catholics were unlikely to involve themselves in such enterprises could hardly succeed with most of the members, and one view that a unity among subjects should be worked for so that 'the Papist and the Protestant can now quietly talk together' appears to have run against the general feeling.[10] The act of 1563, making it treason for certain subjects to refuse to take the oath of supremacy on two occasions, was born in this atmosphere, though some members of the Commons voted against it, possibly because of its harshness. The Queen herself, while apparently disliking the extremity thus offered to law-abiding Catholic subjects, viewed it as a declaration against papal power, 'the common enemy' of the realm.[11] The 'deadly hatred and malice of the papists' was offered as a justification of the subsidy demanded in 1566.[12] Later in 1572 the Ridolphi Plot gave members the opportunity to enlarge upon the problem more graphically, and one of the Kentish members, Sir Thomas Scott, while denouncing Mary Stuart's deeds, said that Roman Catholicism was the principal cause which had produced rebellion, and he claimed that Catholics were in high places throughout the realm, even around the Queen herself.[13] While Elizabeth was not prepared to countenance the drastic action against Mary which Scott and others wanted, more specifically-aimed legislative weapons could be more successful. The anti-Catholic legislation of 1581 was the fruit of the need to protect the country against 'a rabble of vagrant friars', as Mildmay described the priesthood.[14]

Concern for the solidarity of the Church was also evident in a bill first appearing in 1571, and then again in 1576 and 1581. It was an attempt to deal with the subject who refused to attend church, despite the penalties of the Uniformity Act of 1559. Stiff fines were therefore proposed in these bills, but it was also hoped that Catholic subjects would be forced into the open by the requirement to take communion according to the Protestant rite.[15] Prompted possibly by fears of Catholic dissidence after the Northern rising and the papal bull of excommunication on Elizabeth in 1570, it was supported in the Commons in 1571 by Sir Thomas Smith and William Fleetwood, both 'government' men. Fleetwood argued, as did Peter Wentworth was to do in 1576, that laymen, as well as bishops, were competent to deal with God's cause.[16] There may have been some dissentient voices, but the bill carried enough support in both Houses, which explains why it reappeared subsequently. In 1576 it seems the bishops themselves were directly responsible for its introduction. Elizabeth may not have wanted to allow a measure whose proclaimed intent was a high degree of conformity. Since men would be compelled to *participate* in the rite of the Protestant Church, rather than simply attending the services, it might prove divisive, if not impracticable. Certainly one member, Mr Edward Aglionby, had argued that 'it was not convenient to enforce consciences'. In any case, he said, it was impossible to achieve: 'no laws may make a good man fit to receive that great mystery, but God above'.[17]

THE DEMAND FOR FURTHER REFORM

Certainly, Lord Keeper Bacon, who with Archbishop Matthew Parker and Secretary William Cecil has been described as a 'powerful pillar in church and state', seems to have been interested in reforming ecclesiastical discipline. He told Parliament in 1563 that preachers were less diligent than they ought to be, and that there were not enough of them. 'Some of them that be, be much insufficient ... For as heretofore the discipline of the church hath not been good ... The want of discipline causeth obstinacy, contempt and the growing of heresies.' He proposed a remedy which would involve the appointment of officers to redress faults two or three times a year, and said that 'laws [were] to be made for the purpose'. Although he said the bishops 'called together here in Parliament' had the 'chief care' in this, he reminded everyone that any laws which were thought necessary would become matters of parliamentary consideration.[18]

When Bacon said that religion strengthened the State he also spoke of the need to avoid 'superstition', a sentiment shared by those who wanted a thorough reform in the Church. He was careful, indeed, to emphasise the primary role of the bishops themselves, and thus enunciated the Queen's own philosophy, as we shall see. Simply by raising a subject of paramount interest in Parliament, however, Bacon gave the expectation of reform a respectable prominence, and focused attention on the bishops' efforts. As many of the new Elizabethan bishops at this stage were as eager as others to build on the settlement, this seemed reasonable enough. They had, after all, had little or no part in making that settlement themselves. Bacon's words probably helped to ensure that religion continued to be discussed in Parliament for much of the reign. In the process, the bishops lost much of the support they had at the start. This was one of the most significant political features of the reign, and it explains why we should not be too ready to argue that Parliament at this time had no political importance. As we shall see, it was Parliament where the arguments between a supreme governor, and then her bishops, on the one hand, and many of her most important subjects on the other, raged and assumed starkly drawn legal and constitutional dimensions.[19]

The first appearance in 1556 of the so-called 'alphabetical' bills (ranging from A through, eventually, to G) signalled a concern about the quality of the clergy which was to persist well into the reign. They were intended to provide a better qualified and disciplined clergy, which would be freed of the sins of non-residence, incompetence, and the financial exploitation of Church assets. It may be that some, at least, of them originated with the bishops; and there seems to be no evidence that they were a co-ordinated code sponsored by 'radicals', or 'Puritan choristers'.[20] They made no great headway this time, probably because of shortage of time, though their reappearance in 1571 presumably provoked Elizabeth's animosity, and therefore the disappearance of most of them. Without her prior authorisation what was, in effect, a wide-ranging *parliamentary* review of the way the Church was administered and disciplined would not be allowed, for it undermined her governorship. She said she approved of the Thirty-Nine Articles which Convocation had passed in 1563, but it seems she was unwilling to allow Parliament to put its statutory seal of approval to them without her bidding. That had been the intention of what was known as Bill A. It remains true, however, that she did give her assent to Bill B. Since this act set out basic requirements of doctrinal conformity and qualification for clerical office, statutory confirmation of the Articles was achieved. It may be that the general support this measure had attracted in both Houses, together with its stated object of providing for a sound Church, made even Elizabeth reluctant on this occasion to outface her assembled advisers in the Commons and the Lords. Bill E, against the selling of ecclesiastical offices, was also allowed. Many of the bishops had written to her extolling the virtues of the original Bill A in 1566. They had emphasised that the unity of the realm was one of its the tangible benefits, and they said that they had acted because they needed to discharge their souls before God. They were also bold enough to remind Elizabeth that she needed to do the same. In providing that ministers subscribe to the Thirty-Nine Articles (a reflection of Bill A) the act became controversial, because its wording, as we shall see, could be variously interpreted.[21]

This concern about the quality of the Church was not new, and it is hardly surprising that the proposals attracted wide-ranging support in Parliament. Protestants on all sides wanted to strengthen the Church and the realm. Many believed that Catholic priests surviving from Mary's reign needed to be removed and that this was best achieved by requiring them to subscribe to the Articles, backed up by the full sanction of the law. The Queen, however, rejected further statutory involvement in the administration of the Church. For a while the laity's concern about many of the other issues dealt with by the alphabetical bills as a whole took the form of petitions presented to Elizabeth, urging her to redress their grievances. These appeared in the parliaments of 1576, 1581 and 1584–85.[22] The Commons here seem to have been able to co-operate with Councillors in order to approach the bishops and the Queen, though the failure to effect marked improvement led to bitter debates between Queen and subject. This situation was part of the general background of deepening suspicion of the episcopacy among Privy Council and laity which characterised the advent of John Whitgift and his elevation to Canterbury. It must be appreciated that in calling for the reform of clerical abuses, no new agenda was being proposed. No new structures or beliefs were being propounded. In arguing that positive action would bring greater unity among Elizabeth's subjects, and therefore enhance her control of them, her members of Parliament underlined the conservative nature of their proposals, fully in line with the central purpose of parliamentary endeavour as defined by Bacon. Despite these considerations, the Queen's answers continued to display a quality of curmudgeonly and tantalising reproach, and in essence she told the petitioners that the matter could be left to her, if the bishops failed to act on their own account.[23]

By the time Parliament met in 1584, however, this response was wearing thin. There were still identifiable abuses, so the Queen had patently not been willing, or able, to keep her promise. While there had been general agreement between the two Houses on these petitions in 1576 and 1581, the bishops on this occasion recalled that Elizabeth had made it plain that it was the clergy's task to reform these matters, and they told the Commons they would seek her permission before any more was done in Parliament. That was never forthcoming, for Burghley soon had to deliver the familiar royal message. Action would be taken, and Elizabeth said it was good that complaints had been made, because the problems could now be remedied. It may be that her refusal to allow a parliamentary role had been influenced by Whitgift's detection of more radical religious elements in the petitions.[24] Whatever he said in the Lords, the Archbishop also produced an appraisal of the petitions which was intended for the Queen. It was far more scathing than anything communicated to the Commons themselves, and it stressed what he said were the radical, even anarchic, features of the petitions. There can be little doubt, however, that Elizabeth would have wanted to uphold her own authority come what may, even if the petitions carried no suggestion of a Presbyterian alternative to the current Church.[25]

The wide support for clerical improvement can be demonstrated in the session of 1586–87 when proposals for dramatically more radical reform did indeed appear in Cope's Presbyterian Bill and Book. That move was readily blocked, as we shall see, but members' concern about the quality of the clergy persisted in a general discussion of ecclesiastical abuses, a debate in which known Presbyterian members were not prominent among recorded speakers. It was said that 'idolatry' was prevalent in Wales, where the service was said in neither Welsh or English, and the lack of learned ministers was seen by other members as a source of popular ignorance among the Queen's subjects. Sir Francis Hastings, one of the fervent Protestant members, confessed a reluctance to speak for fear of offending the Queen's unwillingness to have religion discussed at all; but he said he was compelled 'by his duty to God, loyalty to the Queen and love to his country'. Better laws were needed so that 'her Majesty may be better obeyed'. Another view was that the bishops were to blame for the unsatisfactory state of the Church and that they 'should be complained on', a notion which Elizabeth later described as a 'disorder'.[26]

In 1589 and 1601 bills were introduced against pluralism and the consequent non-residence of some clergy in their benefices. They thus reflected the long-standing concern which had first appeared in concrete form in the alphabetical bills in 1566. The bill attracted wide support in 1589 and was committed to Privy Councillor Knollys among others, who was particularly anxious that the bishops should be disabused of any notion that they were subject to no earthly control.[27] In the Upper House, Burghley spoke favourably of it, and criticised the bishops for not adequately supervising their staff, while gathering all 'in the purse'. Another temporal peer, Lord Grey, was far more acerbic. He described the bishops as 'enemies to reformation', words which more than anything else tell us how far lay members of Parliament had been disappointed by the failure to develop the Elizabethan Church, and how the bishops had moved on to the defensive. The bill naturally failed to go further, but the voices of complaint had been raised yet again, even in the Upper House which had given this bill a first reading.[28]

In 1601 the story was stranger. There is no certainty about the contents of the original bill, though it probably set out to modify the 1529 act against pluralities – the only other statute relating to the problem, since the bill of 1589 had been stopped – by making them all invalid. If this were the case, then it could have seemed impossibly rigid to some, and amendment became inevitable. Those who favoured it were not averse to changes, but Whitgift's supporters on the Commons committee probably played their part too in softening the original drastic provisions. The measure had thus survived at this stage, and it might have gone forward to the second chamber, as had been the case in 1589. We do not know why this did not happen, and we cannot simply assume that support for the bill in principle had waned. By this stage even the stoutest-hearted fighter for the cause could be forgiven for yielding to the irresistible odds of the Queen's implacable opposition. Anything which had not been undertaken with her privity was generally abhorrent to her, but one of the proposals in the bill was also objectionable in principle. It was that jurisdiction in the matter of pluralities be transferred from the Church courts (the Court of Faculties in this case) to the common law. The Commons committee also appears to have produced the curious situation where the proposed legislation would have enhanced, rather than reduced, the incidence of pluralities. Even the most ardent supporters were able to see that, having attempted to solve the problem on more than one occasion, there was now no real prospect of success with this bill.[29]

It is clear that an active and widely-supported concern about the Church had frequently been voiced, and that it was not merely the work of a small group, or 'choir', of Puritans. Bishops, Privy Councillors, Lords and Commons had wanted statutory backing for an Elizabethan reformation. Men of all Protestant outlooks could fall in behind most of what had been proposed. Queen, church and realm would have been strenghtened in a fulfilment of what Bacon had spoken about in his early speeches to Parliament. Elizabeth disapproved of these initiatives, though not usually because of their substance. Only Elizabeth herself opposed the reformation with steadfast consistency during her reign.

MORE RADICAL PROPOSALS

There were others, however, who urged changes beyond mere adjustments of quality. In 1571 William Strickland, a Yorkshireman with a reputedly sharp tongue, made what was the first attempt at a statutory change to the settlement itself. His bill would have allowed earnest Protestant minsters to deviate from the order of worship prescribed in the Prayer Book.[30] Men like Strickland hoped to move closer to the 'true primitive Church' by dispensing with the 'superstitious' vestiges of the corrupt Catholic past, like the sign of the cross in baptism, and the ring in marriage. If only because it threatened the Prayer Book, a major foundation of the English Church, Elizabeth was unlikely to agree to this. It probably also left supporters of more moderate proposals, like Thomas Norton, cool. Strickland's sequestration on the Queen's orders caused uproar in the House, and Knollys had to explain that his offence consisted not in what he had said, but in introducing a bill, clearly an attempt to smooth feathers ruffled more by Strickland's detention than sympathy for what he had tried to do. Notwithstanding her clear antipathy, another bill, concerning rites and ceremonies, appeared in the next parliament in 1572.[31] Strickland's earlier purpose was reflected in this bill, for it would have allowed ministers (though with their bishops' approval) to ignore sections of the Prayer Book which they found objectionable, while at the same time allowing the prosecution of Papists for deviating from it for *their* own purposes. Treasurer Knollys indeed praised it as a way of remedying shortcomings in the Uniformity Act; but its preamble, which spoke of the need to depart from the 'precise rule and strait observation' of the Prayer Book, would he thought, rouse the Queen's wrath, and he urged amendment.[32] The Queen was intent on killing the bill off, whatever men like Knollys had been hoping for. From the Lords Burghley demanded details of the bill, and in reply, the Speaker made a creditable attempt to commend it. The Uniformity Act was divisive, he said, because it was used in malicious attacks on some ministers who made petty deviations from the Prayer Book. In committee, the preamble was toned down, and the rest of the bill modified; but it went no further than its first reading as a new bill on 21 May. Elizabeth said she was disturbed by the alleged attacks on good Protestants, though *she* would be responsible for defending them. She would discharge her role and defend the faithful; Parliament need not be involved.[33]

The failure of the petitions of the 1570s and 1580s played a part in opening a rift between the Queen's Councillors and her bishops, effectively under John Whitgift's dominant influence since the suspension of Grindal in 1577. Whitgift was mainly responsible for developing the arguments which rejected the parliamentary petitions, while Sir Walter Mildmay, Elizabeth's Chancellor of the Exchequer, blamed the bishops for not implementing reforms to which it was believed Elizabeth was really committed. The development of

Presbyterian views in parts of the clergy and laity inevitably hardened Whitgift and the Queen against any suggestions of change, and Whitgift's battle with Thomas Cartwright in the 1570s alerted him to what he thought were Presbyterian elements of popular election of ministers in the petitions of 1581. Though the petitions were unwelcome to the Queen, the parliamentary Presbyterian campaigns in the 1580s represented the more audacious attacks on her authority.[34]

The plans for abandoning the current state of affairs in the Church and substituting a Presbyterian system in its stead appeared in the famous 'Bills and Books' of Peter Turner and Anthony Cope. It is hard to believe that they imagined that Elizabeth would agree to their plans, in 1584 and 1587 respectively, even if they had initially won the support of the Lords and Commons.[35] Perhaps they thought that the growing dangers from Catholicism would sweep aside even Elizabeth's opposition. Privy Councillors had no apparent difficulty opposing such measures, however, which were no help to the cause being pursued in the petitions. Those who wanted reform do not generally seem to have been part of the Presbyterian drive. Indeed, concern about the clergy readily surfaced again after Cope's moves had been dealt with. Councillors could not be happy with the proposal to rescind all existing constitutions and services of the Church, and Mildmay pointed out that if Cope had his way, the anti-Catholic laws would disappear. The Church courts would also be abolished so that there would be no way to resolve disputes over marriages, the legitimacy of children, and wills. His message was that Cope threatened chaos to men of property and inheritance. This was not the way: there *was* a need for reform, but members of Parliament should approach the problem differently in order to succeed. Cope's Bill and Book had been impounded, and a number of members speaking in support of his action had been arrested, ostensibly for discussing religion outside Parliament. Sir Christopher Hatton parried doubts about the liberties of the House and freedom of speech which had thus arisen, reserving his main energies for an attack on Cope's measures as such. He described Presbyterians as the worst enemies of 'this our reformation'. They would alter the form and order of the Church, he said, rather than reforming the errors. They would replace the comfortable familiarity of the Elizabethan church service with stark sermonising. They wanted to benefit from a transfer of the patronage of livings, and this would be to the loss of many gentry who now enjoyed them. Cope's programme therefore 'toucheth us all in our inherit-ance'. The Presbyterian plan was a body-blow to the whole purpose of *reform* as such, and it compromised security of country and property. The statutory basis of the supremacy would be destroyed in favour of 'pastors, doctors, and elders'. The Queen would, moreover, lose her Church and her revenue from it, and the loss would have to be made good from 'your own purses'. The argument was that the Bill and Book were subversive because they proposed undoing the *status quo* and because the practical, financial and legal consequences were unthinkable. These attacks by Elizabeth's ministers were devastating. 'The pope denieth the supremacy of princes, so do in effect these', said Hatton. In dismissing Cope, they reaffirmed a need for reform, however, and had appeared to sanction the more moderate parlia-mentary action which persisted.[36]

POLITICAL ARGUMENTS

Elizabeth's steadfast opposition to parliamentary initiatives for fur-ther reformation divided her from many loyal members. By this time, however, her position had been reinforced by the appointment of bishops who were more likely to share her conservative tendencies than their predecessors.[37] This was at the expense of exposing divi-sions within the larger political and religious establishment. Privy Councillors squabbled with Whitgift, resented his aggressive ap-proach to disciplining nonconforming ministers, and were rebuked by him. Moreover, the tendency to anticlericalism among the govern-ing classes can only have been exacerbated by the arguments which the Queen used, and which Whitgift deployed on her behalf.[38]

Parliament was an arena for this rift, therefore, where there were not only blocked bills and petitions, but the crossed swords of ideolo-gies as well. This war of words inevitably lacked the lengthy develop-ment and refinement which characterised Whitgift's disputes with Cartwright, but its succinctness arguably gave it greater poignancy. In 1571 the instruction to steer clear of matters of state obviously included religion, because Elizabeth had made her displeasure plain in 1566 when it was raised. After this, Elizabeth's ministers tried to enforce the notion in the House, and both Treasurer Knollys and Comptroller Croft argued that matters of ceremony in the Church were the Queen's prerogative and not to be meddled with. She had been acknowledged to be supreme governor, they said, and it hardly seemed right to 'run before the rule'.[39] In this instance, it probably suited the Councillors to fall in with Elizabeth's line. The issue at stake was, after all, Strickland's bill, and it was of minority, rather than mainstream importance, as we have seen. Under the pressure of continuing interventions in the prohibited territory, the Queen was forced to defend her position further. She showed how far she was willing to go in chastising members of Parliament for their irresponsibility. It was resolute reiteration of the prohibition on discussion, a reinforcement of the message her servants had delivered but which had failed to drive the point home successfully.[40]

Whitgift was hardly less hostile to parliamentary involvement, and he was ready to use suggestions of Presbyterianism to discredit the moderate parliamentary petitions.[41] Elizabeth herself showed no sign of being more yielding to demands for reform simply because members were asking for a better qualified clergy rather than wanting to replace her supremacy with a Presbyterian structure. Her quarrel with members was intense. They were making trouble, she said, by allowing the enemies of the country to characterise it as divided; and they were persistently refusing to accept the statutory basis of the supremacy. She told them, through the Speaker, in 1584–85 that her power was 'next under God; she had full power 'by the law of the Crown', and by the law positive, signified through the act of 1559. She did have, moreover, the will to reform whatever was amiss, so that any action by the Commons was derogatory to her power and distrustful of her good intent. This ought to have been the end of the matter, but members had meddled 'above that that doth become them', despite her commands to the contrary. She made it clear that the mere reception and 'public reading' of the petitions was folly, for the enemies of the realm could now, as a result, pour scorn on her goodwill and ability. The action was all the more objectionable because the matter 'pertained least unto them, being the lowest of the three estates'. There could have been no more explicit dismissal of any notion entertained by the Commons that they had a constructive part to play in reforming the Church. Despite conceding that some things might be amiss in the Church, she insisted that parliamentary discussion of the topic was anti-prerogative and anti-statutory. While men in the Houses were prepared to argue that they were constitutionally correct to base the religion of the land on parliamentary foundations, the Queen used the same foundations to argue that members were acting *against* the law of the land and doing nothing but harm. For Elizabeth, 1559 had recognised a God-given power and strengthened it here on earth; it was the recognition that was parliamentary, not the power.[42]

The severity of this message may have been prompted by what has been called the 'remarkable document' which a Commons committee drew up in response to Whitgift's dismissal of the petitions. Concern about the Church had now been parried on three occasions by half-promises and rejections. Knollys and Mildmay were prominent, by their positions as Privy Councillors at least, on the committee which drafted this document, and Elizabeth made her disgust about this evident. Though the document was not officially presented to her, its mere formulation testifies to the divide which was now revealed, and which gave Elizabeth the opportunity to complain that the enemy could gloat over a Protestant nation at odds with itself. The document complained that the bishops had 'so much forgotten themselves' by appointing incompetent clergy, despite repeated admonitions and despite the act of 1571, which was meant to enhance clerical quality. Promises given in 1576 had amounted to nothing. The Commons were also affronted because arguments in the petitions had been rejected without full explaination. The requirement that the clergy subscribe to all thirty-nine Articles was also resented. Whitgift had claimed they stood 'by law in force', though comprehensive subscription was not required according to some views, as we shall see.[43] Whitgift's demand that ministers should take an oath of canonical obedience was unacceptable because it was not required by 'the laws of this realm, either common law or statute law': the canon law 'is not to be allowed'.[44] Neale repeatedly described this document as subversive, and, from the Queen's point of view, it was.[45] For men like Knollys, however, who were of a distinctively Erastian turn of mind, the intention was not to subvert. It was to prevent the clergy becoming a self-sufficient entity. Wentworth had already told Archbishop Parker in 1571 that members could not allow the bishops to act as popes, as a law unto themselves.[46] When Elizabeth delivered her stinging message through the Speaker it must have seemed that she was in effect supporting that kind of power, and it became evident that conflicting interpretations of the nature and origins of the royal supremacy lay at the heart of the matter.

Ambiguity had surrounded the nature of the royal supremacy since Henry VIII's day, and it had emerged again in defending the settlement against papists and Presbyterians. Some commentators argued that because Elizabeth derived her power as supreme governor from God, Presbyterians had no power to change the shape of the Church. There was also the view that Parliament similarly had no role in the supremacy.[47] The defensive arguments used in Parliament were, however, directed against a broader body of support for reform than that represented by the Presbyterians. Those who felt Elizabeth's wrath were drawn from the political community at large, not just its margins. The Queen herself naturally showed no doubt about the practical meaning of her supremacy. A draft message prepared for Parliament in 1587, probably in response to a further petition for clerical improvement, was headed, 'Why you ought not to deal in matters of religion', and a pithy section declared, 'Her Majesty taketh your petition to be against the prerogative of the Crown. For by your full consents it hath been confirmed and enacted ... that the full power, jurisdiction and supremacy in Church causes, which heretofore the Popes usurped and took to themselves should be united and annexed to the imperial crown of this realm'.[48]

Certainly Elizabeth's sharp riposte in 1584–85 seemed to make the prospect of open division between Queen and subject a reality. Though some suggested that the petitions on the clergy had been kept from her, and that she was thus innocent of members' frustration, there could be no doubt that she was set firmly against Parliament's dealing with religion. Having come to this point the members had to ponder carefully, for no one could treat such a prospect with indifference. Indeed, it was agreed that the Commons must uphold their position. A bill which would have reinforced the provisions of the 1571 act for better ministers was submitted and reached a first reading in the Lords. There, no less a figure than the Earl of Leicester supported it with the argument that a functional review of existing legislation was a valid task for Parliament to undertake. Vague or weak statutes, he said, properly came within the compass of Parliament's powers.[49]

There were others keen to pursue this line in Elizabeth's later years, though she would not allow their efforts to succeed. From the start of the reign many had been disappointed about the apparent lack of fervent Protestantism in the Prayer Book and the Thirty-Nine

Articles. The Queen's drive for a uniformity of clerical dress and the bishops' role in implementing it in the 1560s left the Church with further stress. On top of this, the 'alphabetical' act of 1571 concerning clerical 'disorders' required ministers to subscribe to the Articles. It used to be recognised that this act embodied a victory for zealous Protestants in the Commons, for the text of the final statute said that ministers should subscribe to the Articles 'which only' concerned the faith and doctrine of the Church, and that they were therefore not required to accept the others. Another interpretation suggests that the phrase was not intended to allow the clergy to subscribe *selectively* to the Articles at all, but had been inserted as a palliative, explaining that subscription was acceptable because the Articles did nothing other than assert the doctrine of the Church. Nothing untoward was therefore being required of the clergy.[50]

It is not clear why a palliative was necessary at all, however, and uncertainty about this act remains. The purpose of the measure was to purge the Church of the old surviving Catholic priesthood, and it may have been sufficient to use the test of the explicitly doctrinal Calvinist articles for the purpose.[51] One does not need to imagine that 'Puritan' members were impatient with bishops because they were thought to be blocking further reform, and that they therefore wanted to weaken those Articles which dealt, for example, with matters like the consecration of bishops. It is true that Peter Wentworth said in 1576 that members of the Commons were not prepared automatically to endorse all the Articles simply on the Bishops' recommendation. This circumspection about prominent clergymen is hardly surprising or novel, and it offers no certain help about what happened in the case of this bill. On the other hand, another, also retrospective, view of the bill's passage claimed that the intention *had* been to limit subscription. Whitgift's strict requirement of adherence to *all* the Articles (as well as the Prayer Book) seemed to require an acknowledgement that the Church had no fundamental faults, and it became a test which Whitgift wished to use extensively.[52] The act of 1571 came under close scrutiny, and Robert Beale for one railed against the bishops' attacks on nonconforming ministers. In the course of a long attack he appealed for support from members who had taken part in passing the act. 'I pray you that were of the House ... when the said Articles were confirmed, to call to your remembrance how when the subscription to the said Articles in the first draught of that statute was somewhat general, you yourselves thinking the words too captious caused the subscription to be restrayned to the Articles of faith only.'[53]

The question of how far the Church was to be subjected to the law of the land thus became major a concern for men in Parliament; and try as she may, Elizabeth was unable to ban discussion. In 1589, Humphrey Davenport, a young lawyer member, urged the necessity of tying the bishops to the law by preventing them from using the *ex officio* oath and imprisonment in their drive against ministers who would not conform. Four years later, James Morice, another lawyer, and Attorney of the Court of Wards, introduced two bills which proposed the same things. It was felt that neither practice had a standing in law; and these moves were not part of any Presbyterian vision of a *new* Church. Davenport's 'motions' which he proposed as the basis of a conference between members of both Houses, bishops and judges, were a mixed bag of old complaints about clerical incompetence and lingering traces of 'idolatry', not least the retention of the wedding ring and the sign of the cross in baptism. So much had been on the agenda from the start of the reign, and the stated purpose – as in the early years – was further reformation and consequent means of unity in the nation. Morice's bills were a defiant rejection of Elizabeth's oft-repeated instruction on religious matters, but they attracted the support of other members, including Knollys himself, so that the House called for a reading. The Queen was forced yet again to order the discussion to cease.[54]

A FANATICAL COMMONS?

To the extent that Parliament's behaviour over religion was a problem for the Queen, the role of a narrowly based 'Puritan' group is minimal. Indeed, the Puritan 'fanaticism' which Neale believed had informed many proceedings was far less pronounced than he believed. The trouble for Elizabeth arose because significant numbers in Lords and Commons wanted to purify the Church further. It was majorities rather than minorities which made the Commons a potent threat in Elizabeth's reign. It is also important to stress that when bills concerning religion and its protection from Catholic foes came up, reasoned debate occurred, and that questions of practicality and necessity were considered. The general criteria for making laws were not left to one side because the safety of Protestantism was on the agenda. It will not do to see Commons or Lords gripped by passions to the exclusion of rational common sense. For example, in 1571 a bill for reform of the Court of Faculties came before the Commons and would have prevented the Archbishop of Canterbury dispensing with the canon law, 'contrary to the word of God'. It fell foul of the House, however, though it ought ostensibly to have done better. It reflected the layman's suspicion of clerics by seeking to reverse the Henrician Act of Dispensations of 1534 by which the 'Bishop of Canterbury is made, as it were, a pope, procured by the bishops at that time'. The Court of Faculties seemed to be doing nothing to discourage the pluralism and other clerical abuses which were a constant cause of complaint. None the less the bill failed, and there is nothing to prove that the Queen herself had stopped it. There *is* evidence, however, that members of the Commons were not happy that it could achieve its aims. It was said that its scope was unclear, or too general. Given that 'in the making of laws two things are to be considered, the grief and the remedy', the grief was obvious, although the remedy was not. As drafted, the bill required that to secure a conviction the Church should, in effect, admit to a 'temporal judge' that it had granted dispensations contrary to the word of God. This was beyond imagination. It looks as though these practical objections necessitated a complicated redrafting, and the bill foundered because of shortage of time.[55]

These considerations also help to explain what happened in 1593 when anti-Catholic bills were under consideration, and when, it has been argued, there was less fanatical 'Puritanism' and a more tolerant attitude towards Catholics than had been evident, for example, in the act of 1581.[56] These bills were both officially inspired. The bill concerning recusancy was introduced into the Commons, but what eventually emerged as an act to retain subjects 'in their due obedience' was the result of a second bill, this time starting life in the Lords. In its complicated passage the Commons expended much energy on curbing the dangerous parts of this bill against recusancy. It originally proposed to extend the clause of the 1581 act which made it treason to absolve subjects from their loyalty, or to be absolved by those who attempted this, so as to penalise separatists. Protestants could thus be brought within the scope of the law, which would also have banished recusants not conforming after three months' imprisonment for their non-attendance. While no sympathy for the Protestant separatists was expressed in the Commons, members were worried that the measure's loose drafting would entrap other Protestants who were not wilful separatists. This concern was reasonable enough, but the objections to the bill were articulated by members as lawmakers, not just as anxious Protestants. One complaint was that by extending the 1581 act to separatists, 'schisms' became equated with sedition and treason. Separatists could therefore be seen as having withdrawn their loyalty. It was also said that loose phrasing was a danger to those who merely discussed controversial matters such as excommunication and pluralism in the Church.[57] Men who were not guilty could suffer, as Raleigh said; and he also questioned the appropriateness of death or banishment as penalties where juries would have to determine whether there had been an *intention* to withdraw subjects from their natural obedience. Others said that if sectaries – Brownists and Barrowists – were the targets of the bill, then they should be defined. The changes which resulted reflected these doubts. Most notably, the clause referring to the 1581 act and invoking its treason penalty was excised, and as much as possible was done to shift penalties away from zealous Protestants, who might simply absent themselves from church in protest at incompetent ministers, and specifically towards separatists. Protestants had every right to protect themselves from what seems to have been an attempt by Whitgift to arm himself with powerful legislation, but he was arguably unwise to enter battle with a Commons adept at asking the right questions when making any law, let alone one which would strengthen an unpopular cleric. In this way the story of this act is not so different from what had happened in earlier days.

Similar concerns had already arisen when the earlier bill, which this measure had replaced, was debated. The Commons wanted the extensive penalties proposed for 'recusants' to apply explicitly to popish recusants only. These penalties were extremely harsh. Land and goods would be forfeited on a large scale; Catholic children would also be taken from their families and brought up under offical supervision; and recusants would not be allowed to sell, buy, or rent land. There was no obvious provision for restoring land in the event of repentance. A clause against harbouring recusants was thought to be too loosely drawn, possibly because some members had recusant wives and wanted therefore to protect themselves. The bill may also have seemed to be a threat to property rights. As the committee later decided, 'the husband not being a recusant to forfeit no part of his land for his wife's recusancy'. All in all, the measure threatened very severe penalties, and the committee's reaction to it says as much about the practice of lawmaking as it does about a new-found tolerance towards Catholics. One member had doubted the propriety of removing all means of livelihood from recusants so as to deny them a living.[58] The provision was removed because it was 'too hard'. Otherwise the penalties were softened and the dangers which could arise from harbouring recusants were reduced, especially with regard to recusant wives.[59] The proceedings in this bill have been compared with what happened in 1581, when the act against Catholics was passed. Then, it is said, the Queen intervened to soften penalties, but it was the Commons who were the more lenient twelve years later, and that roles had therefore been reversed. It is significant, however, that the starting-points for the two bills were not identical, for the 1593 measure was more draconian than what was first contemplated in 1581. Neither is it clear that Elizabeth had tempered the earlier proposals, though she may have been happy about the outcome.[60] It is equally likely that the legislation of 1581, as in 1593, was the product of disagreement, resolved by debate and committees, among members and Councillors themselves about appropriate levels of penalisation. In such matters, there was a constant interplay of the more or less passionate with the more or less prudent.

The so-called 'Five-mile' Act of 1593 was another example of an officially-prepared bill – this time clearly against Catholics alone – being modified and softened. This Lords bill was an attempt to neutralise the possible seditious activities of certain Catholics by controlling their movements to within five miles from their homes, and it threatened them with loss of goods and income for straying further. If an offender had no land, he was liable to lose his life. It looks as though the committee in the Lords, where the bill was introduced, reduced the death penalty to banishment, and other clauses were also toned down. Despite all these changes, these acts continued to provide penalties for Catholic recusants which remained harsh by any standards. The removal of banishment as a penalty for popish recusants from the act for obedience has also been regarded as a sign of greater tolerance. Yet the Five-mile Act must be viewed alongside this, for under its provisions, banishment remained a possibility for obstinate Catholic recusancy.

The Church did not undergo the changes which many of Elizabeth's subjects desired. It could be argued that Elizabeth came out of her dealings with Parliament rather well as far as religion was concerned. She had defended her supremacy throughout, and strengthened it with further laws. The extreme Presbyterian attacks of the 1580s had been defeated without much difficulty, and may, indeed, have bolstered her hold because they underlined how preferable the status quo was to the proffered alternative, That was presented as an attack on stability, family settlements and property itself. She had hardly benefited, however, from a spirit of co-operation as far as the nature of the Church was concerned. Indeed, what Parliament saw was rather more co-operation between Lords and Commons, at the expense of the supreme governor. Her later troubles were arguably eased by virtue of her later episcopal appointments, and after the 1570s the bishops' involvement was not what it had been. Equally, though the splits over issues of Church reform towards the end of the reign are limited and embryonic rather than severe, they were significant. The supreme governor of Church and State defended her position by drawing the lines more positively against all comers, but there were those in the process who found themselves being asked to straddle an uncomfortable divide.

NOTES

1 Jones, 'Religion in Parliament'.

2 See *PE*, p. 198 and n., but also Loach, review of Jones, for persistent doubts about Elizabeth's own wishes.

3 Jones, *Faith by Statute*; Dickens, *English Reformation*, pp. 353–61; Guy, *Tudor England*, pp. 260–2.

4 Jones, *Faith by Statute*, pp. 50–4, 83–103.

5 Collinson, *Elizabethan Puritan Movement*, p. 35; Collinson, *Religion of Protestants*, pp. 31–2.

6 Haugaard, *Elizabeth and the English Reformation*, pp. 185–200; Dickens, *English Reformation*, p. 359.

7 *Procs.*, pp. 34–5, 47.

8 *EP*, ii.424.

9 *Procs.*, pp. 81, 91–2.

10 *Procs.*, pp. 101–2.

11 *Procs.*, p. 111.

12 *Procs.*, p. 142.

13 *Procs.*, pp. 349–50.

14 *PE*, pp. 178–81; *Procs.*, pp. 499, 505.

15 *PE*, pp. 201–3.

16 *Procs.*, pp. 201–2; Graves, *Elizabethan Parliaments*, p. 73; see Chapter 7.

17 *Procs.*, pp. 205–8; *EP*, i.192–3, 349.

18 Collinson, 'Sir Nicholas Bacon', pp. 266–9; *Procs.*, pp. 70–1, 80–2.

19 Russell, *Causes of the English Civil War*, p. 87.

20 *PE*, pp. 205–14, and references there.

21 Jones, 'Religion in Parliament', pp. 121–2; Bruce (ed.), *Correspondence of Matthew Parker*, pp. 291–4.

22 *PE*, pp. 214, 216; *EP*, i.349–53, 398–404; ii.61–4; Collinson, *Elizabethan Puritan Movement*, pp. 162, 187, 282.

23 *Procs.*, pp. 445–7, 510–21.

24 *EP*, ii.65–6.

25 Lambeth Palace Library MS 2002, fos. 53–7.

26 Collinson, *Elizabethan Puritan Movement*, pp. 311–12; BL Harley MS 7188, fos. 93v–4.

27 Cargill Thompson, *Studies in the Reformation*, pp. 105, 118, 126–8.

28 *EP*, pp. 227–9.

29 *EP*, ii.406–10.

30 *Procs.*, pp. 200–1, 220.

31 *Procs.*, pp. 330–1, 362–3.

32 *Procs.*, pp. 368–9.

33 *PE*, pp. 214–16; *EP*, ii.297–304.

34 *EP*, i.404–5.

35 *EP*, ii.62–3; D'Ewes, *Journals*, pp. 410–11.

36 BL Harley MS 7188, fo. 96; BL Sloane MS 326, fos. 112–21; PRO SP 12/199/1.

37 Cross, *Royal Supremacy*, pp. 60–1, 107; Lake, *Anglicans and Puritans?*, p. 92.

38 Collinson, *Elizabethan Puritan Movement*, pp. 162, 201, 256–7, 258–9, 271, 281–2; Lake, *Anglicans and Puritans?*, p.72; Guy, *Tudor England*, pp. 307–8.

39 *Procs.*, pp. 220–1.

40 *EP*, i.173.

41 Lake, *Anglicans and Puritans?*, pp. 63–4; *Procs.*, p. 511.

42 BL Harley MS 6853, fos. 285–6.

43 See p. 96, this chapter.

44 Northants CRO: Fitzwilliam of Milton MS, Political 2, fos. 23v–24.

45 *EP*, ii.72–3.

46 *Procs*, p. 432.

47 Scarisbrick, *Henry VIII*, pp. 392–4; Cross, *Royal Supremacy*, esp. pp.
    35–6; Lake, *Anglicans and Puritans?*, pp. 64, 135–7, 211–12.

48 Lambeth Palace Library MS 178, fo. 88; *EP*, ii.162–3.

49 *EP*, ii.77–83.

50 Collinson, *Elizabethan Puritan Movement*, pp. 34, 36, 66; *PE*, p. 213.

51 Hughes, *Reformation in England*, iii.157–9, 195 and n.3.

52 Collinson, *Elizabethan Puritan Movement*, pp. 248, 281–2.

53 BL Additional MS 48116, fo. 162v – Beale himself was not a member
    until 1576; see *EP*, i.390 for another example of limited subscription
    proposed in the 1581 Bill against Catholics, though excised.

54 Longleat Bath, Thynne MS lxxvi, fos. 7–8, 11; *EP*, ii.273, 278.

55 See Chapter 2; *Procs.*, pp. 222–3; Jones, 'Religion in Parliament', pp.
    127–9.

56 See *EP*, ii.280–97, and esp. 296 for these measures.

57 BL Cotton MS Titus, Fii, fo. 88v.

58 BL Cotton MS Titus, Fii, fo. 34.

59 BL Cotton MS Titus, Fii, fo. 26v.

60 *PE*, pp. 186–7; *EP*, i.386–90, 393.

Chapter 6

Lords and Commons

One of the serious consequences of the belief that a political struggle characterised the relationship between Elizabeth and the Commons is that too little attention has been paid to the other House of Parliament. It may not be possible, however, to reconstruct a picture of the Lords which is as detailed as that of the Commons, simply because the surviving evidence of the Lords' proceedings is meagre in comparison. A number of points can, however, be usefully made about the Upper House and its relations with the Lower. The Lords obviously enjoyed a cachet and prestige which arose from its venerable origins as the great council of the kings of England. Although commoners, representing counties and boroughs, had sometimes joined them, the 'lords' continued to sit in the Parliament House and made it their own, the Commons only gaining access to the Palace of Westminster in the middle of the sixteenth century. It was in the Upper, rather than the Lower House that the Queen sat when she joined Parliament, and it was here that the Lord Chancellor, or the Lord Keeper, presided and instructed the Commons, assembled at the bar of the Lords itself, to nominate their Speakers. It was a small, select establishment, being drawn from the titled aristocracy and the episcopacy of England, and Henry VIII's reformation, by removing the abbots at the dissolution of the monasteries, had reduced its size to a total of eighty or so potential members by the beginning of Elizabeth's reign. The Queen's well-known parsimony in granting new honours did little to change this, for there were only ten elevations to the peerage in the course of her reign; and the six attainders for treason – mostly after the rising of 1569 – have to be set against these, as do other losses arising from natural causes. The House was thus an intimate body whose members, if they remained alive and in office, were far less subject to change than the Commons, whose composition was determined by an electorate and some competition for seats, however limited.[1]

This lack of turnover in membership may have given the House an important practical edge over the Commons: theoretically, it meant more continuity of experience in the business of making laws. Yet the contrast with the Commons needs to be qualified, for although the membership of the Lower House expanded, and was subject to substantial change at each election, there were men who became regular fixtures on the scene. Cecil, Hatton, Mildmay and Knollys are merely the most obvious Privy Councillor members who between them sat on twenty-six occasions, though most of William Cecil's parliamentary service was in the Lords, from 1571 to 1597 inclusive. Men like Fleetwood, Yelverton and Norton also made twenty-four sessional appearances in the reign. All these might be described as 'men of government', and along with the Privy Councillors in the Commons formed an active 'presence', though not perhaps always self-consciously acting as such. Yet there were many other members who could claim a respectable record of membership. About one-third of the members in Elizabeth's reign sat in more than one parliament, and there were thirty-one who sat in more than six, twenty-nine who were sent up for six, while no fewer than 401 were returned for three, four or five parliaments. Since some of these parliaments consisted of more than one of the thirteen sessions of the reign, the figures underestimate the degree of continuity. On the one hand, then, we can say that about 20 per cent of the members of Elizabeth's Commons went back to Westminster for no less than three, or up to six, parliaments; or we can say that less than half of each House had been there in the preceding session, though for three of the parliaments the proportion was nearly as low as a quarter, and for most, below 40 per cent. Others, however, may have sat in Parliament other than the one immediately before.[2]

Rarely, if ever, were the full memberships of the Houses present. In the case of the smaller House of Lords, it may be that numbers who attended in practice made for a compact and effective working body. Having said that, the same practical considerations should be applied to the Commons. To complain of its unwieldiness because of its size, and of its inefficiency because of absenteeism, may be to single it out for unfair criticism.[3] The absence of many members of the Commons (indicated by division figures) is not wholly satisfactory as a guide to the commitment and activity of members. For one thing they do not tell us anything about the contribution to business made by the many committees appointed to deal with the scrutiny and amendment of bills. Concentrating the attention of the House through a much smaller body of minds was obviously a sensible way of conducting business, as well as saving the time of a hard-pressed House. Though attendance at committees could also be so thin as to impede effective business, committees remained an obvious solution to the problem of scrutinising and amending bills. Moreover, it looks as though attendance rates – how large a proportion of each House attended every day – was roughly the same for both Houses. The Commons appear to have had around 33 per cent of its members present usually as a minimum, though nearer half of the total membership may often have been in the House. In 1559, attendances in the Upper House in early February ranged from twenty-nine to forty-eight,[4] while in 1584–85 there seem generally to have been between thirty and fifty members present, more usually at the lower end of this range; and the same was roughly the case for 1601.[5] Not that these figures necessarily tell the whole story, by any means. The information on the Commons is taken from division figures which occasionally appear in the journals as well as diaries of proceedings, and the Lords' attendance registers presumably record appearances at the beginning of the day. Needless to say, such attendances in both Houses are snapshot measurements, and were subject to considerable variation throughout the day as members came and went about their business. It is equally true that though members of the Lords could register a proxy at the start of a session, appointing a proctor to stand for them, they were not prevented themselves from attending in person thereafter. It looks as though, on most days, a handful of peers might have registered their attendance, at least, though they had earlier appointed proctors.[6] It may be true that a greater *proportion* of the Lords in fairly regular attendance were involved in government, and therefore had a direct interest in being there, but it is by no means clear that *fewer* members of the Commons similarly involved – albeit a House five times the size of the Lords – bothered to turn up.[7]

The lords were summoned individually by a writ enjoining them to consider urgent business concerning the Queen, the State, and the defence of the realm, as well as the Church. Thus the charge was the same as that which went down to the towns and counties for the election of the burgesses and knights.[8] The sovereign's practice of telling the Lords and the Commons jointly, in the House of Lords itself, about the tasks facing the coming session of Parliament reinforced the notion that the realm, gathered here in its constituent parts, was engaged in a common task. These matters were to be dealt with by both Houses, each of them being places where counsel was to be given, 'wherein all men are bound to discharge themselves'. The Lord Keeper's instructions were delivered to 'my lords and masters all', though Bacon was careful in 1563, as we have seen (see Chapter 5) to stress that the bishops were responsible for the discipline and doctrine of the Church. Any legal adjustments which were to be made in consequence were to brought before Parliament's consideration. Thus all men of Parliament, lords, bishops, knights and burgesses, were jointly commissioned to advise and assist, and though, as we shall see, some matters appear to have fallen to one House rather than the other, there was no general division of tasks between the two chambers.[9]

THE IMPORTANCE OF THE LORDS AND COMMONS

The Commons' growth in importance in the late medieval period is best illustrated in the recognition that its participation in the making of law was necessary, yet the essential involvement of the Lords was obviously *maintained*. Nobody imagined that the Commons' arrival as a maker of laws was at the absolute expense of the other House, or that it became sufficient of itself for the process. Since the Upper House was able to initiate bills itself, and engage in all the same stages of passing and rejecting measures as the Commons, then it is plain that historians' unease about its neglect is justified. Yet there seems to be no doubt that most of the bills coming before Parliament started life in the Commons.[10] In purely quantitative terms therefore, the House of Lords could be seen as the minor part of the bicameral institution, but the obvious point that all legislation had two Houses, not just one, to go through underlines the practical importance of the Lords in lawmaking. Since bills were subject to all the processes of scrutiny – readings, commitment, amendments – in both Lords and Commons, wherever they had started life – the Lords' actual role of determining the nature of laws was no mere formality. The amendments which the Upper House made to Commons bills were often accepted, as were the Commons' changes to Lords' measures.[11] As far as the Council was concerned, it is difficult to detect a principled preference for one House against the other. Major bills were often introduced in the Commons in the early years when Cecil was there, though the Lords also played its part. Later on a shift in the Commons' favour may have occurred, though the Lords were never left out of the business of launching government bills entirely.[12] On the other hand, the continuance bills, which gave life to acts which would otherwise lapse, were usually introduced into the Commons. In this way the Commons appears to be the point of departure for legal (and thereby administrative) continuity. Though William Cecil spent much of his parliamentary career in the Upper House he seems to have done nothing of a lasting nature to reverse the long-term decline of the Lords as the main initiator of major legislation. While the Lords' share in the initiation of acts seems to have fallen as the reign proceeded, the Commons appear to have retained an overwhelming predominance in the initiation of bills, at least. Probably about three-quarters of all bills were introduced in the Commons.[13]

Both Houses were thus necessarily involved in law review, but their relative importance has been debated by historians. It is not easy, however, to find a wholly satisfactory means of measuring this, either by determining which House handled the greater number of bills in the first instance, or by gauging how many of such measures became acts. What mattered at the time was that the progression of business between the Houses was completed. It is true that in some cases one House rather than the other was seen as being more appropriate for some measures. Bills for the restitution of titles started life in the Lords, while those for naturalising individuals were introduced into the Commons.[14] This was customary, and very little, if anything, of constitutional significance ought to be deduced from it, other that that this was the way in which the constitution worked for these particular purposes. Generally, there seems to have been no fixed rule, and the fact that most bills started in the Commons reflects contemporary choice rather than constitutional necessity or significance. The business of introducing a bill and taking it through both Houses was an expensive one. It was obviously a matter of judgement for a group of cloth manufacturers, for instance, whether it made sense to bring a bill to the Commons first, where the real battle with other interest groups might be fought, and won or lost, most vigorously. Troubles from the second House in each case may have seemed minor battles once any initial skirmishes had been overcome. In any case, though the Lords handled fewer measures than the Commons, one of its strengths was that it enjoyed the services of a number of legal assistants, judges and law officers who did not vote.[15] These were able to cast a professional and watchful eye over both Lords bills from their earliest stage and over many more Commons bills at a later stage – when presumably some of the more glaring errors had already been detected and ironed out. They thus helped to ensure, as far as possible, that all legislation satisfied general criteria for making law espoused by the Lords Keeper and members of both Houses alike.

It may not be very helpful either to attempt to determine the 'importance' of the House on the basis of its work-rate or efficiency. Measuring rates of success by determining the number of acts which resulted from a given number of bills introduced into the respective Houses may seem attractive, and on this basis the Lords in the mid-Tudor period has been adjudged more productive and successful: 'The productivity – *and therefore the success* – of parliaments can *only* be measured by the enactment of statute.'[16] The individual successes of the Lords clearly depended on the co-operation of the Commons and vice-versa, simply because neither House was capable of making law on its own. Moreover, if the Lords were so clearly superior as lawmakers we have to discover why so many men persisted in putting their measures into the Commons. The notion also assumes that a bill must become an act before we can talk of Parliament's doing its work well. Clearly from the point of view of individuals, official or otherwise, who had particular proposals to get through, the measure of success was a statute at the end of the day. It cannot be stressed too much, on the other hand, that law review, rather than law production, was the overriding principle, so the mere fact that some bills failed to become laws does not mean a failure of the parliamentary process. Parliamentary statutes gained their legal and moral force from the supposition that all had assented to them. They had passed the test of scrutiny, where pros and cons had been heard and assessed. Review – examination, and action if necessary – was the important point, not mere productivity. If measures appeared to be unredeemable by amendment, then it was necessary to reject them. Rejection was a sign of effective parliamentary work if it followed from careful scrutiny, because a decision was taken on the suitability of the proposal. Rejection was bound to be an important part of the process of sifting wheat from chaff. This, then, is a major problem in itself, even before we attempt to solve the thornier problem of deciding if all bills and acts are 'equal', for unless they are – and they are patently not – then comparisons of figures cannot provide the whole answer.

CONFLICT BETWEEN THE HOUSES?

The foregoing is the necessary basis on which we must consider the question of the relationship between the two Houses, a relationship which has often been dominated by notions of friction and conflict. The mere fact that Parliament functioned as a bicameral assembly explains why the two elements could genuinely fall foul of each other.[17] It is not easy, in fact, to find much evidence of 'collisions' in which a genuine desire to achieve a constitutional edge over the other House was apparent, or to identify any political thought which would have given rise to it. It is not always clear, moreover, when a collision was a real one or merely a temporary hitch which could be resolved, given a predisposition by both Houses to work together.[18] This is not to say that each House, each part of the procedural machine, was not capable of feeling affronted by the other; or feeling that its freedom to operate had been endangered by the ignorance, incompetence or sheer presumptuousness of the other House. To assume that even the last of these shortcomings derived, however, from a conscious desire to encroach on the 'political' domain of the other party may not be warranted. It is just as likely, after all, that any touchiness between the Houses came from a serious belief that as each was obliged to approach its legislative tasks responsibly, each naturally believed it had the skill to do so. Professional pride, rather than constitutional precociousness, is probably the key to a proper understanding of the situation here then.

In the normal run of things, relations between the two Houses could be affected by a number of factors. It is not really surprising, for example, that mistakes occurred from time to time. An assembly which met only irregularly, and then for a short period, was liable to trip up sometimes on the technicalities of procedure and protocol.

Yet there was also a flexibility in the way the machine worked, which was one of its assets, and it emphasised the commitment of the Houses to make things work. For instance, in 1576 the Council wanted to legislate so as to reduce the number of offences which could qualify for benefit of clergy. This was achieved by an act which originated in the Lords. The part which removed rape of children under ten years old from the scope of benefit may have been added at the last moment by means of a Commons proviso, though with the specific agreement and, indeed, urging of the Lords. This was appropriate as a prominent Commons member, Recorder William Fleetwood, had wanted legislation on this point long before this parliament met. In this case, the sequence of steps by which measures passed from one House to the other meant that the Lords had been unable to add the provision themselves, though they were clearly willing for the Commons to do so.[19]

In 1581, sheer forgetfulness on the part of the Commons' clerk about these procedures probably added to disagreements already existing between the Houses about the bill for seditious rumours.[20] More obviously, however, difficulties could sometimes arise because newly appointed officials were sometimes liable to make mistakes through lack of experience. In 1597 the Lords sent back some Commons bills which they wanted to amend. There was nothing wrong with that, for it was clear that changes were possible, even though the bills had reached the point where the first House had debated them and ironed out problems to the extent of indulging in the expensive process of engrossing them in parchment. What should also have been clear, however, was that the Lords' suggested changes ought to have been written on a sheet of paper and sent down so as to allow the Commons' clerk, whose handiwork the parchment engrossment was, to make the changes to the document himself. The Lords' clerk, newly appointed to the job, had arrogated this task to himself, and the Commons' man explained that he had told him what to do on an earlier occasion when he found him committing the same errror. This indulgence explained, incidentally, the fact to which the Lords had objected, that the Commons had raised no protest when it had happened before. The incident reminds us that we are dealing with human institutions, run by individuals liable to individual frailties. We can even understand why the Lords, confronted with the Commons' rejection of their parchment amendments, grew tetchy and retorted that it did not really matter whether they were on parchment or coloured paper.[21]

The scrutiny to which bills were subjected was understandably meant to reveal imperfections in drafting, though there was no guarantee that all shortcomings would emerge in one House so that the bill entered the other in a state of perfection. The Forests and Apparel Bills of 1576 nicely illustrate the working relationship between the two Houses. Starting life in the Lords, the bills caused problems in the Commons for a number of reasons (see Chapter 2). When the Houses conferred in joint committee the Lords' representatives agreed that the Commons' criticisms had some merit, and that the bills had been inadequately drawn. They even told the Commons to go away and suggest changes of their own in the case of apparel. The fact that the two Houses were later to find themselves unable to agree on final versions, and that the bills therefore failed to become acts in 1576, indicates no more than that: there was no talk of the Lords having exceeded their powers according to the Commons, or vice versa, no hint, in other words, of pressure arising from conflicting concepts of relative roles in the constitutional or political process.[22]

Mundane considerations, rather than constitutional struggle, were also at the root of the famous incident over the subsidy in 1593. On this occasion the extraordinary grant of three subsidies was made, though the initial suggestion came from the Lords, not the Commons itself. It may be that Elizabeth and her ministers had not clearly determined the level of taxation to be requested on this occasion, but in approaching the problem in this way they blundered. By this time the principle that the Commons initiated tax grants was well established and should not have been questioned, given the urgency for revenue. It was not even as though there was any real advantage to be gained or lost by not allowing the proposal to surface first in the Lower House. In that way, the notion that the subsidy was the 'free gift' of the subjects, as Elizabeth liked to call it, would be preserved. After years of granting single subsidies, the novel recourse to two subsidies in 1589 had caused no *great* problem, and so it is all the more puzzling that the issue was not tackled in the same way in 1593, by airing the subject in the first instance in a Commons committee.[23] Again, in the end, despite the Commons' legitimate complaints about procedure, the tax demand of 1593 was agreed to. This was only after the correct *form* had been followed, so that it could appear that the proposal had actually come from the Commons; and Burghley had to explain that he had only urged the House to *consider* an increased grant. It was important that the correct form be followed. Though the idea may have come from other quarters, as arguably it had always done, the process had to remain within the House, otherwise part of its *raison d'être* was lost, and its role was diminished. In so far as we are dealing with a 'tussle' on this occasion, we are dealing with one which had arisen because of the Lords' insensitivity, rather than a Commons wish to carve themselves a bigger place in the constitution (see Chapter 3).

'Professional' pride could lead to touchiness, and because pride was not the prerogative of the Lower House, it might sometimes appear that the the Lords, rather than the Commons, could be the assertive element in the equation. Thomas Norton himself saw that there was a danger of the Lords dominating the Commons, especially by means of joint conferences. In the case of Stourton's bill, his anxiety was reinforced when the Lords asked for a conference, even though practice indicated that it was not their place to do so, because the bill was not in their possession at the time (for Stourton, see below, this chapter). By 1581 the Commons agreed to the precaution of stipulating – at Norton's behest – that their committees should not assent to anything suggested to them by the Lords' representatives unless it had the specific endorsement of the whole House. Again, as far as Stourton's case was concerned, the Commons were keen to preserve the notion that any measure, whether signed, and thus recommended, by the Queen or not, should be judged on its merits. This was a point accepted at the time by the Lords but apparently denied by Burghley nearly ten years later.[24] As it was clear that money bills were to be intitiated in the Commons, the episode in 1593 might also have amounted in practice to the Lords' pressurising the Commons into granting additional taxation. However clumsy the incident was in 1593, there was no suggestion that the Commons had to accept the Lords' proposal. In the end the formal location of the initiative remained in the Commons, wherever the idea had originated. The theory that tax grants came from the Commons and were assented to by them was upheld.

In these ways, the Lords could, perhaps, be as 'pushy' as the Commons are often said to have been. This may lend some weight to the view that Cecil's move to the Upper House in 1571 saw an attempt to control the Lower. Neale was surprised that the Commons did not object to the Lords taking on 'a larger share than usual in initiating the main bills' in 1571 when so much time had been spent on the 'alphabetical bills'.[25] The surprise can only be justified if we believe that the initiation of legislation necessarily represented political or constitutional virility, and that its absence therefore signified impotence. It is more likely that because the bills on religion, supported now, it seems, by many in the Lords in any case, had taken up considerable time and it made sense to start necessary business in the Lords rather than the Commons as was the case with the measure for the continuance of statutes.[26]

Even if procedural technicalities and drafting were not problematic, however, it was not necessarily plain sailing thereafter. The fact that the two Houses were part of the law review process, and that neither was really a rubber stamp for the other, meant that differences on matters of principle were liable to emerge. Clearly there could be disagreements *within* each House, for this is what debating, and taking votes in divisions, was meant to resolve. They could equally arise *between* the Houses. Just as it was possible for a bill to sink within one House because of disagreement over content and principle (with or without going to a vote), so the hurdle which slowed progress, or even killed a measure stone dead, could arise in the second House. To recognise this obvious point goes a long way towards explaining what occasionally went 'wrong' between the two Houses, without having to believe that such difficulties were constitutional tests of strength. There are examples where there was demonstrably disagreement between the Houses about how to conduct business. On such occasions there may even be evidence that one, or both, of the Houses its collective dignity had been affronted. This only emphasised the fact that each of them believed that theirs was a vital, though not *the* vital, part in making law, and that its integrity had to be preserved.

The measure brought into the Lords by Lord Stourton for his restoration in blood provides one of the best examples of 'trouble' between the two Houses. Stourton wished to limit the consequences for him of his father's conviction for murder. Being summoned to sit in the Lords in 1576 was one important step, but he had also secured the Queen's endorsement on a bill which would allow him to uphold his title to lands. The question which emerged was simply whether

Stourton, son of a murderer or no, should be allowed to capitalise on any errors in the land deals of his father or other forebears, whether, in other words, parties exchanging land with his father could lose land because of any legal irregularities in the conveyancing process. The Commons wanted to add a proviso which would prevent Stourton from bringing writs of error to do this, and so protect those who had dealt with his father. The Lords believed this was an unnecessary precaution, and suggested the Commons had erred in tampering with a measure which had the Queen's support. This also caused resentment, because the Lords seemed to be trying to tell the Commons how to deal with a measure which had now passed into their domain. Mildmay and Norton, both 'government' men, were prepared to argue the case from the opposite side of the fence against Burghley himself. More importantly, it was probably folly to attempt to bully the Commons on an issue involving property, of all things. The disagreement over the clause itself was fundamental and principled. The Commons were adamant about the proviso, and on this issue the measure foundered. They probably did have the right to propose alterations to measures of whatever nature they were, and Stourton's bill was not immune simply because it carried the Queen's personal recommendation in the form of the sign manual. This was one of the principles they upheld at this point, and it was against what seems to be a manifest attempt by the Lords to favour Stourton's cause. It was not Commons' self-aggrandisement, however, that we see here. Neither was the House merely reacting spitefully to the Lords' recent rejection of its own bill against errors and recoveries, designed to prevent the sort of fraudulent practice envisaged in Stourton's case. In that bill the Commons showed their commitment to an important principle, so its loss was important, and we should not be surprised that, seeing the principle go down in a general measure, they should uphold it in a particular one. They were not, arguably, singling Stourton out for particular attention because they had also tried, in the case of another private bill, to deny Anthony Mayney the chance of exploiting errors to others' disadvantage. To see the episode as small-minded, patent foot-stamping is to miss the point that the Stourton case is a prime example of irreconcilable differences of principle between the two Houses, and that this led to a failure to make law.[27]

Disagreement over principles was always a possibility. The government bill against fraudulent conveyances, originating in the Lords in 1584 and said to be a measure particularly favoured by the Queen herself, caused enormous problems when it reached the Commons. Its attempt to outlaw fraudulent practices in the sale of lands was another in a series of attempts to regulate aspects of the land law. The bill proposed to allow Star Chamber a jurisdiction over these matters. Many in the Commons disapproved, and one prominent member likened Star Chamber to a serpent. The Commons were so displeased with the measure, in fact, that they eventually proposed reframing it themselves, a suggestion which the Lords accepted. As a result the proposed Star Chamber competence to deal in matters of property was jettisoned. The Commons had clearly considered the whole measure as initially framing an unsatisfactory answer to a problem which everyone recognised and wanted to solve, but as one speaker in the Commons said of the original bill; 'Here we go about to remedy a mischief with an inconvenience.'[28]

The complicated story of the act against recusants and sectaries of 1593 provides another good example of a first-class battle of ideas between the two Houses. Despite the political ascendancy which Whitgift apparently enjoyed at this point, it is not clear how much he was able to achieve. More to the point, perhaps, differences existed within, as well as between the Houses. There could, after all, be no reason to suppose that there would be unanimity among a group of men simply because they sat in one House. It looks as though the Lords were not at one, for Burghley may have been unhappy about the proposals, and others became concerned about the possibility of being fined for their wives' recusancy, a concern also voiced by some of the Commons. The bill had its supporters in the Lower House who resisted moves to moderate its scope and harshness. At a crucial point later on, Vice-Chamberlain Sir Thomas Heneage plainly attempted to mislead the House so as to retain as much of the substance of the new Lords' bill against the hostile Commons committee. Cecil also bludgeoned the Committee into agreeing to the measure though, in the end, it still retained a dangerous element.[29]

QUEEN AND LORDS AGAINST COMMONS?

Another possibility to be considered is that the Lords was seen as a means of controlling the Commons, and that the Stourton bill was, perhaps, a case in point. Indeed, because the Lords was so small, Elizabeth might have been able to use it as a block on the troublesome Commons. Outward appearances do not readily suggest, however, that this was so. In the first place, her sparing use of honours meant that she denied herself the opportunity of packing the upper chamber with tame political creatures. The point at which this might have happened was after the resignation of the Marian bishops, so that she had the opportunity to refashion the House to her liking. This arguably worked against her as much as for her. Her first generation of bishops played their share, as we have seen, in the 'trouble' over religion in Parliament in the earlier years. Later on, when the tougher, more conservative bishops took their places it is by no means clear that they were able to exert a controlling influence over the Commons, and Whitgift's difficulties in 1593 were real. His answer to trouble which he saw coming from the Commons was to rely on the Queen's authority, rather than the Lords' (see below, this chapter).

If the Queen pinned her hopes on a wholly 'loyal' House of Lords then she was frequently disappointed. Early in the reign they combined with the Commons in attempts to force her hand in her own affairs. Far from lending support to her in some way, they had ranged themselves with what she thought of as unruly elements in the Commons. Here was a beleaguered Queen who looked very disturbed and alone. In her father's time, as she reminded them, Parliament had been an occasion for demonstration of unity within the regime.[30] It might have seemed to the Queen that whatever he wanted had become his. Yet already by 1566 members of the Lords were probably behind the spirited attempts to reform the new religious regime, and the House had joined with others to compel her to act on the question of her marriage and the succession.

Burghley's arrival in 1571 did not make a noticeable difference, for the Lords continued to be willing to sympathise with some of the Commons' encroachments into areas unacceptable to Elizabeth. Though in the end the Houses did not agree to joint action on the benevolence in 1587, the mere fact of a Lords' offer of money over and above the subsidy seemed to associate them with the Commons' earlier wish to pressurise the Queen over the sovereignty of the Netherlands. Even worse, perhaps, was Burghley's involvement in the plans to provide for an interregnum in the event of the Queen's

117

death, a reflection of a measure possibly considered by the House in 1563. The lengthy story of progress towards the death of the Scottish queen arguably marks an epic parliamentary struggle which stretches back to 1571 and witnesses the periodic parading of political differences on a grand scale. Under these circumstances the Lords' importance was immense: the Commons recognised it, and that is why the two Houses worked so closely together over issues such as this.(see Chapters 3 and 4).

These were clearly important issues because they were seen as sacrosanct by the Queen, yet there were other important areas where the Houses could undoubtedly represent a constitutional, even political threat to the Queen. Despite the fact that she controlled the final tally of bills which became acts at the end of each session, there are cases where Elizabeth came under severe pressure. In 1571, the very year of Burghley's arrival in the upper chamber, the Lords were prepared to take an ostensibly threatening position over the prerogative. This was in their support for a bill which had emerged from a Commons committee, and which would have controlled fees charged by Exchequer officials on tenants-in-chief for respite of homage. The broad similarity of social and economic interests between Lords and Commons had produced agreement between the Houses, and it looks as though the Queen was forced to intervene to stop the measure which would have imposed statutory controls over Exchequer officials and their inquiries into the affairs of the landholding gentlemen of England.[31] Another instance was the famous Sedition Act of 1581. This sought to provide a better means of dealing with propaganda aimed at the Elizabethan religious regime, and was based on the act of 1555, designed to protect Mary Tudor from hostile words. One of the problems about this Lords' measure is that we do not have precise information about the nature of the Commons' objections to the proposed penalties. Neale imagined they wanted to scale them down so as to reduce the danger the act would present to 'Puritans' from the fate which had befallen John Stubbs for producing a pamphlet against the proposed match between Elizabeth and Alençon. It seems odd, however, to imagine that a measure so weakened in one respect could have been considered effective in the other, namely dealing with Catholic slanderers. Yet there may have been a more straightforward objection to the measure than this, for it is clear that the Commons detected drafting problems. The bill provided that engaging in certain activities would constitute guilt, whereas the Commons appear to have insisted that safe convictions should follow only if an *intent* to dishonour and slander the Queen could be proved. Whether the intention was to protect Protestants by making enforcement more difficult, or simply to make convictions safer at law, the objection carried an important point of principle and policy. When the Lords attempted to undo it the gulf of ideas between the Houses was merely underlined. In the end both of them seem to have yielded ground. Elizabeth may not have wanted to allow the Commons to reduce the penalties and prevent their enforcement against Protestants, but it is not clear that she thought the act necessary at all, and may have thought it absurd. In the end, she assented to it with some reluctance. The Lords, who behaved throughout as though they really wanted it, do not appear as loyal executors of the Queen's will.[32]

Though the story of the bill for the better keeping of the Sabbath in the parliament of 1584–85 is an example of a measure where the two Houses initially disagreed over precise detail, by the end of the session there was accord, and Speaker Puckering made a special point of commending the bill to the Queen for her approval: he had already applauded two measures, those providing for the Queen's safety and against Jesuits and seminary priests, which had enjoyed the 'great and mature deliberation' of Lords and Commons. Since, he continued, 'all good laws of men ought to be grounded upon the eternal law of God expressed in the second table of his ten commandments, and calling to their remembrance what godly and Christian laws your Majesty hath already published' – against Catholicism – the Lords and Commons 'have thought it their parts to go forwards, and by providing for the rest and right use of the Sabbath day to provoke your Majesty to give law concerning the 4th and last commandment of the same table also'.[33] Though he may not have delivered this section of his speech in the event, this attempt at 'provoking' the Queen to move 'forwards' by the combined forces of the Commons, the Lords and Almighty God could not prevail against the Queen's omnipotent prerogative in this sphere. The two Houses did, however, try again in 1601 with a milder measure, which this time disappeared after two readings in the Lords.[34]

Several years later, in 1589, the Commons wanted to resurrect the matter of purveyors. Both Houses had agreed on a bill in 1587 (which the Queen had stopped), and now another bill, newly passed, was in the Lords by 25 February, along with another, the Exchequer Bill, which touched the prerogative. This was intended to solve grievances, among other things, over Exchequer officials' use of the writ *quo titulo ingressus est*, another area where landholders felt a degree of financial harassment. In the Commons it had gained the support of the Chancellor of the Exchequer himself, as well as his chief official, also a member. All in all, this looked like an opportunity for constructive reform arrived at by co-operative deliberation between Commons and the Exchequer itself. Within two days Burghley, acting on the Queen's instructions, asked the Commons to meet the Lords and subsequently told them that the measures were unacceptable. It may be that the Lords themselves refrained from reading the Commons' bills out of respect to the Queen's patent aversion to them, though the *Lords Journal* naturally does not tell us this. It is, perhaps, more likely in view of their apparent ready support for the Commons two years earlier, that Elizabeth's speedy intervention was prompted by the need to prevent a repeat of the joint action on the Purveyors' Bill. Burghley was, after all, to refer favourably to the proposal two weeks later in his support of the Commons' Bill on Pluralities.[35]

Though the action on the Exchequer ground to a halt in 1589, a bill did pass the two Houses in 1601. It clearly marked the persistence of former complaints which had surfaced as long ago as 1571, and then again, as we have seen, in 1589, and it drew attention to the fact that the Queen had promised reform, rather than agree to the legislative curtailment of her prerogative. Yet again in 1601 Elizabeth had not changed: it was *semper eadem* and she vetoed the bill. This action also, incidentally, threw up another 'incident' between the Houses about to which of them should be responsible for amending a proviso added by the Lords. It seems that there was genuine doubt all round as to procedure here, though this did not ultimately prevent an agreement that the Commons should do it.[36]

It is hard, on the other hand, to enumerate many examples where the Queen was able to throw the weight of the Lords against the troublemakers, as she professed to think of them, in the House of Commons. We know, for instance, that there was sympathy from some of the House for the Commons' petitions on the state of the clergy in the 1584–85 parliament, despite Whitgift's opposition.[37] Perhaps the most telling comment on Whitgift's role in the Lords is his plea to the Queen to help. In 1585 he faced a Commons bill for the better enforcement of the 1571 act relating to the clergy. This had been passed in defiance of the Queen's rejection of their intervention in religious matters, and he seems to have genuinely feared that the Lords would actually pass the renegade bill. It is not clear that the Queen could take the House for granted too often: and it seems that Whitgift could not rely on their lordships to neutralise pressure from the Commons, but had to rely on the Queen's direct intervention.[38]

It is important to stress at this point that the number of bills Elizabeth vetoed does not necessarily provide a good measure of political friction between Queen and Parliament. It may be that Elizabeth only deployed the royal veto on a few occasions; but this quantitative approach may be misleading on its own. As we have seen, it looks as though Elizabeth sometimes stepped in before bills which threatened her prerogative had completed their passage through the Houses, and it may not have been wise to deploy the veto, a very 'public' rejection, on too many occasions. The Queen, after all, made much of the folly of revealing divisions between herself and her subjects in Parliament. It is also instructive to consider the nature of the vetoed legislation. Though the tally of bills Elizabeth rejected in the first half of her reign is small, it contained some of the most important issues of the day: the bill touching the Scottish Queen; a bill on purveyors (encroaching on her prerogative); and a number of attempted interferences with the royal supremacy. In all these ways both Houses showed a willingness to trespass on royal terrain, and the riposte was that they should not pass.[39]

The Lords' support was not automatically available to Elizabeth and this was an important factor in some of the main areas of political controversy. Her displeasure at the way in which her lords spiritual and temporal behaved, in 1566, for instance, was clear. As far as the serious problem of monopolies was concerned in 1601, the Lords were obviously powerless to do much at all to help the Queen, even if they had been inclined to do so, for the issue never arrived with them. Neither her Privy Councillors nor her bishops behaved wholly as her creatures, and it must have seemed to her that the 'natural' props of her regime were not wholly reliable.[40]

There is a view that the relationship between Lords and Commons was shaped by patronage links between the great landowners in the upper chamber and the clients whose election they may have supported, or helped to secure in the Commons. Thus the social pre-eminence of the Upper House was translated into an institutional and political superiority. This issue has not yet been fully explored, and it remains to be demonstrated whether the conduct of individual members of the Commons was effectively prescribed by virtue of owing election to a member of the Lords. It is said that the common line apparent in 1572 over Mary Stuart is an example of the political manifestation of such links, as is the large number of members who were clients of Burghley and Bedford in particular.[41] In 1572, however, since Elizabeth was one of the few who did not believe in taking action against Mary, we cannot read too much into the appearance of a virtual political unanimity against her. Neither did the undeniable social links between members of the two Houses prevent disagreements within and between Houses, as we have seen. A recent study of the Earl of Leicester and parliamentary clientage does not suggest that he was assiduous in attempting to influence elections, or that he secured election for 'his' men in order to control seats, or exert significant influence in the affairs of Parliament. It begins to look as though members participated because of their own inclinations, 'not because they were the instruments of faction'.[42] Where electoral influence existed it was probably a function of the *mechanics* of political life in Elizabethan England, how men became members, not what they did when they arrived at Westminster. The clientage links are most obviously a reflection of the social cohesion of the small section of society which provided the governing men of England. It is this cohesion which helps to explain why there was a large measure of intellectual and political solidarity between the Houses on issues which Elizabeth was most anxious to keep to herself. It also emphasises that men of both Houses were governors, bred up to rule the realm and make its laws. This did not necessitate that every member of Lords and Commons be an enthusiastic participant, but it did mean that the two parts of the tripartite being which was Parliament shared a common point of existence, and that this in itself could produce sparks as as well as harmony.

NOTES

1 Graves, *House of Lords*, pp. vii, 1–8; *EP*, i.40–1.

2 *EP*, ii.23, 194; *Commons*, pp. 39, 81–2.

3 Graves, *Elizabethan Parliaments*, 31–4.

4 *LJ*, i.544–50; *EP*, i.40.

5 E.g. *LJ*, ii.63–70, 80–7, 228–46.

6 Cf. Graves, *Elizabethan Parliaments*, p. 32.

7 *EP*, i.31; D'Ewes usually gives attendances for the start of business each session: not uncommonly, there were more than fifty. On the three occasions when figures are drawn from later in the sessions they are markedly lower, as low, in fact, as twenty–five: D'Ewes, *Journals*, pp. 62–3, 96–7, 140, 197, 227, 267, 313, 319, 377, 422, 456–7, 523–4, 535, 599.

8 D'Ewes, *Journals*, p. 2 and cf. Montague in 1559 in *Procs.*, pp. 8–10.

9 *Procs.*, p. 82; D'Ewes, *Journals*, p. 11.

10 *PE*, p. 94.

11 *PE*, pp. 111–12.

12 *PE*, pp. 92–3.

13 Graves, *Elizabethan Parliaments*, pp. 70–1; *Tudor Parliaments*, pp. 123, 139 for 50 per cent acts originating in the Lords in 1571, the proportion thereafter failing, though the Lords remain the more 'productive' of the two Houses; *PE*, p. 93.

14 *PE*, pp. 91–2.

15 *PE*, p. 88.

16 Graves, *House of Lords*, p. 174.

17 See Graves, *Elizabethan Parliaments*, p. 54 for 'tetchiness'.

18 See e.g. *EP*, ii.59 (Sabbath Bill of 1585), 54, 234.

19 *PE*, pp. 63–6.

20 See below, pp. 118–19 this chapter; *PE*, pp. 90, 188; *EP*, i.396: Elton appears to attribute the bill's difficulties to the self-importance of both Houses, though this seems to underrate the serious problems involved.

21 D'Ewes, *Journals*, pp. 575–7 and reference there to a further incident on pp. 562–3.

22 *EP*, i.355; *PE*, pp. 272–3, 284–6; *Procs.*, pp. 448–51; 454–6.

23 *EP*, ii.205–6.

24 *PE*, pp. 115–17, 355–7.

25 *EP*, i.235.

26 *PE*, 143–6; even so the Commons received the Treasons Bill (*EP* i.225–6) as well as that for fugitives overseas (*PE*, p. 184).

27 *PE*, pp. 116, 337; *Procs.*, p. 533.

28 *EP*, ii.84–8.

29 See Chapter 5; *EP*, ii.280–7, 288, 290–1, 294; *LJ*, ii.182, 184; *CSPD* 91–4, p. 341; D'Ewes, *Journals*, p. 513.

30 See Chapter 4; *Procs.*, pp. 122, 148, 162; *EP*, i.142–3.

31 *EP*, i.219, 224; *PE*, pp. 102–3, 123.

32 *PE*, pp. 123, 188–90; *Procs.*, p. 544; *EP*, i.393–8.

33 BL Lansdowne MS 115, fos. 38, 40.

34 *EP*, ii.60, 395; *LJ*, ii.248, 251.

35 *LJ*, ii.134–5; *EP*, ii.210–11, 228.

36 *EP*, ii.419; *LJ*, ii.254–6; D'Ewes, *Journals*, p. 616.

37 D'Ewes, *Journals*, pp. 344–5.

38 *EP*, ii.78, 81, 83; see also 228–9, 273, 283–91, 357, 408–10.

39 *PE*, pp. 125–6; see Chapter 5.

40 See Chapter 5; *PE*, pp. 201–3.

41 Graves, *Elizabethan Parliaments*, pp. 29–31, 52–3.

42 Adams, 'The Dudley clientage'.

Chapter 7

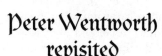

Peter Wentworth revisited

There has been little change in views about the nature of Peter Wentworth's speeches and interventions in the Commons. The idea still seems to hold good that Wentworth was striving for free speech in the wider sense, claiming that the members of the Commons had a constitutional right to initiate debate on any matter without let or hindrance from the Queen. However, he has been increasingly seen as a lone, unrepresentative, and idiosyncratic figure whose importance is far less than once imagined.The rest of the Commons, it is argued, were occupied pre-eminently with their lawmaking activities. There was no general inclination to follow Wentworth's quest for a freedom of speech which would place the Commons at the dynamic centre of the constitution, or a wish to assume a central position in the politics of the day. Because Parliament is no longer seen as the cockpit of political conflict, Peter Wentworth has, perhaps necessarily, been relegated to the sidelines of the story.[1]

A number of questions have to be answered if we are to arrive at a full understanding of Wentworth's significance. We need to know what he was saying and what moved him to say it; and we need to consider what this tells us about his place on the parliamemtary scene. As far as Wentworth's motivation is concerned, the traditional view has been that as a 'Puritan' he was concerned to push forward the course of religious reformation in Parliament. It was argued that, before 1587, he perceived that the way to victory for the Puritan cause depended on establishing a widely defined parliamentary liberty of free speech. After 1587, however, privilege ceased to be uppermost in his mind, and he became absorbed in the problem of the succession.[2] It was accepted, therefore, that there was a fundamental shift in his ambition, and while the proposition is by no means implausible *per se*, it does require that the shift is justified and explained. At first sight this is not easy, for Wentworth appears to have had little direct part to play in religious agitation in Parliament. It is true that he was involved in the negotiations over the bill concerned with the Articles of religion in 1571 (see Chapter 5), but apart from this he cannot be shown to be a religious 'campaigner' in the way that other members like Strickland, Turner, Cope, and even Norton obviously were. In 1571 Strickland was detained because of his bill for amending the Prayer Book. What seems to have agitated Wentworth in this session, however, was the misrepresentation of Robert Bell's intervention on royal licences.[3] We know that this still rankled in 1576, when he made his famous interrrupted and half-delivered speech.[4] Again, in 1581, there is no record of Wentworth having complained about the Queen's order to stop meddling in matters of religion or that he was subsequently active in religious matters.[5] There remains the Presbyterian activity of Anthony Cope in 1587, and Wentworth's connection with it. This might be the climax of Wentworth's assertion of parliamentary free speech untrammelled by Elizabeth's attempts at restriction, but even here, as we shall see, we need to be circumspect in explaining what triggered his participation. Indeed, apart from this, one might be forgiven for wondering why Wentworth was ever thought of as a religious campaigner. Naturally the state of the Protestant religion was of paramount importance to him. His speeches testify well enough to the strength of his religious belief, but he was by no means unique in this respect. To many it seemed that the danger to Protestantism would be reduced if Elizabeth settled the succession. Towards the end of his career Wentworth's concern was *patently* the succession to the English throne; but we need to examine the importance of his comment that he had first been 'stirred up to deal' in the matter of the succession in the early 1560s,[6] and to determine what motivated him to pick up the cudgels in 1576 and launch himself into the long-prepared, half-delivered speech which caused his imprisonment in the Tower at the apparent behest of the Commons itself.

The verdict on Wentworth depends largely on this speech, on the account of his interview by the Commons committee on the same day, and on the questions he wanted the Speaker to put to the House in 1587, supposedly as a challenge to the Queen's action against

Cope's Bill and Book. The speech has never been thoroughly examined. Although Neale dealt with him on more than one occasion, the
content of Peter Wentworth's thought was not subjected to critical
analysis. In *Elizabeth I and her Parliaments*, barely a page was offered
in support of lengthy passages quoted from the speech itself, and
phrases almost as ringing as Wentworth's own were used to assert
the notion of Wentworth's contribution to the quest for England's
liberties. Here, and in the case of the famous unasked questions of
1587, the documents were being asked not only to speak for themselves but *by* themselves. This is important because it can be argued
that the speech is far from clear. Closer examination is needed before
we can accept the verdict that Wentworth's contribution was the
'distillation of the revolutionary endeavour and excitement of the
Commons' into 'simplicity and clarity', inappropriate for 1576 but
'hallowed by the future'.[7]

THE 1576 SPEECH

For the sake of convenience we may divide the speech into four
sections. The opening part proclaimed the benefits which flow from
free speech. A long second section dealt with the 'impediments' of
free speech, namely rumours and messages in the House, and there
was then a substantial argument which demonstrated their wickedness, with a short pithy coda on the duties of members, as Wentworth
conceived them, 'according to the writ we are called up by'. A short
third passage condemned the way in which two-faced members
spoke one way but voted the other. The fourth part was a polite wish
that the House take Wentworth's speech in good part as a token of his
goodwill and concern for the prince and State. It was during the long
second section that Wentworth's comments about the fallibility of the
Queen led to his being silenced. Thus although his words about the
benefits of free speech, along with the notion that it was granted by a
special law to which the Queen was subject, were presumably delivered, the parts of the speech which are arguably the more trenchant
did not reach the Commons' ears, at least directly.

Neale saw that the opening section set out the 'commodities' that
flow from free speech, yet he interpreted Wentworth's *description* as a
claim that Parliament ought and must deal with matters of royal and
state security. Wentworth repeated the description in 1587 when he

said that Parliament is the place where 'all wounds, sicknesses and sores may be cured'.[8] The points made here do not seem to constitute an argument about the limits of free speech, because Wentworth is simply concerned to enumerate its benefits. In any debate a full disposition of the case at hand, with the pros and cons freely argued, was a necessity. Only if debate were conducted in this way could falsehood be exposed and truth stand revealed; and only in this way could important laws for weighty causes be effectively made. It is also significant that, apart from an early reference to matters concerning 'God's honour', the preoccupation is with the health and safety of the prince and the realm, and the perils threatening them.

When we move to the second section about rumours and messages problems begin to arise. Wentworth's language is often dramatic at the expense of precision, and the drift of his argument is elusive. The main burden of the speech is to be found here. Wentworth started with the verses from Job about wine in new bottles bursting forth and the consequent need, as he saw it, to try to do good, rather than going about merely to please people. His intention is to prove that the bearers of rumours and messages were guilty of mischief and wickedness, and that they deserved to be punished. Rumours of the Queen's displeasure (or pleasure), or messages hindering (or promoting) discussion are a dishonour to the Queen. She is bound to uphold the liberties of Parliament, freedom of debate in this case, since they are a part of 'the law', and the law provides the foundation of her own position. Rumours and messages also dishonour members, for they suggest that the Queen distrusts them, otherwise she would want 'all things dangerous to herself' to be discussed. Debate should be pursued according to the merits or otherwise of the matter in hand, and not with a view to 'dissembling as eye-pleasers'. When Wentworth argues that 'we ought to proceed in every case according to the matter, and not according to the prince's mind', he is most obviously arguing for frank debate rather than for any notion of Commons, or parliamentary sovereignty over its agenda. He then entered on a minor homily about the supremacy of law over princes, citing the standard part of Bracton to clinch his point. He concluded that free speech, which is a part of 'the law', must be upheld by the prince: 'free speech and conscience in this place are granted by a special law', said Wentworth in one of many memorable phrases.[9]

Neale gave this notion a central role in his account, arguing that

Wentworth here claimed for free speech 'a fundamental entrenched place in the constitution', and implicitly that it was consequently free from the prince's definition: 'it was immune from legitimate interference from the Crown'.[10] Wentworth was cutting no new ground here, however, for the Commons had already described their privilege this way in 1566, and the Queen had denied any intention of infringing it. The concluding part of this passage on rumour again concentrated on the need to be able to air all opinions without running the risk of being seen as unfaithful, a charge as unacceptable to Wentworth as the denial of free speech itself. When he spoke of the Queen conceiving an evil opinion of her 'faithful and loving subjects' he appears to have reflected what had been Speaker Bell's unrest at the end of the session of 1572. On that occasion, Bell had asked that the Queen think well of members who had spoken frankly in the debate on the bill for her safety. They cared for her preservation, he said, and they did not wish their words to be offensive 'whatsoever hath been or shall be reported to the contrary', an observation which drew the retort from the Queen that he was worrying about nothing.[11]

Wentworth was clearly incensed about rumour-mongers who had done the Queen and her members of Parliament a disservice. Do his words support the notion that he was pushing members' rights into new constitutional terrain? Certainly, he tried to demonstrate that it was possible for a prince to be evidently wrong on occasion, and he argued that at such times there was a duty to disagree. This was justified by what appears to be a concept of members' duties to their constituencies and the country, a theory of representational imperatives, in other words. 'We are chosen of the whole realm, of a special trust and confidence by them reposed in us.' If the prince favoured 'a cause perilous to himself and the state', members had a right to refuse to 'follow the prince's mind'. Wentworth did not explain what 'following the prince's mind' means, and it is not clear whether he was merely elaborating his argument that speech should be free, or frank, or if he wanted something much bigger, namely the freedom to determine the nature of the agenda. His device of resorting to biblical and other allusions by way of demonstration of the point is no help, for they merely concentrate on the evils of flattery, and make the point that whosoever opposed Elizabeth's wishes for the sake of preserving her should be considered to be an 'approved lover'.

Similarly, it is not clear in this attack on rumour whether Wentworth wanted to deprive the Queen of her veto on the discussion of religious matters. 'If we be in hand in anything for the advancement of God's glory', he said, almost hypothetically, it would be wicked to say the Queen wished us to stop, and he hoped she never would want to do so. 'The Lord grant this thing may be far from her Majesty's heart.' Again, Wentworth does not say the Queen would be wrong or acting illegally. His verdict is wickedness, and the sanction divine, rather than terrestrial and constitutional. Neither is it clear whether he envisaged a discussion which had been initiated independently, or one which had been approved by the Queen to start with, and which had then simply got out of control.[12]

When he moved on to messages, however, Wentworth made ostensibly more explicit claims. By recalling that an instruction had been given in 1572 not to discuss religious matters, he appears *prima facie* to be saying that the Commons *should* be the arbiters of their agenda, and it is arguably the point where Wentworth's claim to constitutional originality is most apparent. He asked: 'Is it not all one thing to say, "Sirs, you shall deal in such matters only", as to say, "You shall not deal in such matters"?' Accepting such messages, and 'taking them in good part doth highly offend God, and is the acceptation of the breach of the liberties of this honourable council'. Curiously, this section of the text was never printed by Neale or Elton. Wentworth attacked the notion that the bishops enjoyed a monopoly of the Holy Spirit: 'Seek ye first the kingdom of God ...' is an injunction, he said, for us *all*, and he justified this position by an appeal to the nature of the parliamentary writ which was the basis, he thought, for all members' service: 'the writ we are called up by, Mr Speaker, is chiefly to deal in God's cause'. Wentworth's answer is to 'hate all messengers and tale-carriers or any other thing whatsoever it be that any matter of way infringes the liberties of this honorable council'. Is this the point where we can see Wentworth's religious concerns generating revolutionary constitutional thought?[13]

It is important to keep the sequence of ideas clear, because the burden of this long, complaining speech is subjected to protracted development. The injunction to abhor messages follows Wentworth's development of his earlier argument about the safety of the Queen, and his recollection of an episode in 1571 concerning the bill for the confirmation of the Articles of religion was crucial to this argument.

He and other members had been deputed to hear Archbishop Parker's comments on the Commons' handling of the bill, and Parker had asked why some of the articles had been left out. Wentworth had claimed that shortage of time was the reason. It had not been possible to examine how the articles in question accorded with the Word of God. 'We will pass nothing before we understand what it is, for that were to make you popes. Make you popes you list, for we will make you none.' Wentworth was here most obviously concerned with the necessity for the Commons to scrutinise fully any bills which had been placed before them. They should not be a mere rubber stamp or talking-shop and accept without question the dictates of the bishops.'⁴

It was this experience which led him to believe that the bishops were responsible in 1572 for the message that there should be no discussion of religious matters. While this obviously was a matter of regret in its own right, Wentworth's first concern was with the *result* of the bishops' action. A substantial part of this section therefore becomes a specific treatment of the events of the 1572 session of Parliament. The wickedness of messages was demonstrated, he says, by the subsequent unsuccesful quest for legislation to deal with Mary Stuart in that session. Being forbidden to discuss religion was an affront to God, and some men had said prophetically that the business of the Scottish queen would be blighted. God had been 'shut out of doors', and so Elizabeth had been induced by God to turn down measures framed for her own, and the realm's, protection. It was this action which showed the Queen's errors which would endanger herself and her subjects. Members themselves, as we shall see, had special grounds for fear as a result.

Somewhere at this point Wentworth was silenced, and so the more *theoretically* challenging part of the argument was denied the House. His view was that Elizabeth had summoned Parliament 'to prevent traiterous perils to her person, *and for no other cause*'. He did not complain about the limited parliamentary agenda, and his frustration sprang directly from its being curtailed from the Queen's own starting-point. In this poignant part of the argument, Wentworth asserted that Elizabeth's change of direction had produced not only a sense of anxiety among speakers as to what they could safely say in the course of a debate initiated by the Queen herself, but a personal threat to members from other quarters. Failing to deal with Mary Stuart clearly exposed the nation to the continued danger of plots, but this was not all. The confident expectation engendered by Elizabeth's instruction at the beginning of the session had been that the Scottish queen would be dealt with by specially-tailored legislation. They had expressed themselves freely about what should happen to her, and Wentworth himself had apparently descibed her as 'the most notorious whore in all the world'. More than one member had called for her early death, Thomas Norton seeing it as the necessary precursor to the settlement of the succession. Elizabeth then dashed all hopes, and Wentworth believed that the enemy abroad would benefit because of the failure to protect Queen and realm. The danger was greater than this, though, for speakers in the debate had 'deciphered' themselves to her Majesty and 'our hateful enemies'. The fact that no progress had been made had left them in the lurch: 'has not her Majesty left us all to the open revenge?' Wentworth's hope at this point was that Elizabeth would respond to sound counsel, that 'will may not stand for reason'. The wickedness of messages was here starkly revealed in Elizabeth's 'abuse' of her nobility and people in Parliament.[15]

This was a complex speech, which ranged over a number of areas concerned with the scope of parliamentary debate. Wentworth's argument may not have been that anything could be legitimately discussed by members at their own determination – a point he did not, as we have seen, clearly establish – but that the Queen ought not send messages forbidding discussion on matters which were properly part of the agenda. Certainly he was not happy that religious discussion had been banned in 1572, but he always knew that what was guaranteed to bring his downfall was his view that Elizabeth had wronged her subjects. It is understandable that his language provoked a strong reaction in a House which had always believed that speech should be kept within the bounds of reverence, and in a situation where Privy Councillors would be lashed by Elizabeth's tongue if they failed to uphold some discipline in the House.

Wentworth was subsequently examined by a Commons committee which wanted to know how far he believed messages could be attacked. The account of this examination is his own, and Wentworth not surprisingly appears to acquit himself with creditable strength of purpose, even to the point of humbling, if not humiliating, his interlocutors. If we expect to find one of the supposed architects of English liberties seizing the opportunity here to clarify his views, however, we are disappointed. In the first place, the committee undertook to question him in detail only on that part of the speech which he had actually delivered in the House, even though they had access to the full text. Thus Wentworth was not examined on the point at which he had apparently regretted the 'acceptation of a breach of the liberties' of the House by receiving the message not to deal in matters of religion. Secondly, Wentworth shed little extra light on what he had said in his speech, even choosing to repeat many of the original words in answer to the committee's questions.[16]

The dialogue certainly flowed in such a way as to give him the chance of clarifying his beliefs, for the committee expressed surprise that he had been hostile to messages, presumably when he referred to the 'doleful message' about religion. 'You may not speak against messages, for none sendeth them but the Queen's Majesty.' Wentworth replied that this could only hold if 'the glory of God', the safety of the prince and the 'liberty of this parliament House' were not impugned. Indeed he even insisted that the precedents, apparently produced by the committee at this point, ought to be discounted because they were 'evil'. Wentworth is clearly talking about the message to cease discussion on religion, but when asked to explain why he had made 'so hard interpretation' of messages he repeated the relevant part of his speech almost verbatim. The committee professed amazement that he had said that it was dangerous for the prince to abuse his or her nobility and people, and wanted to know how he had dared to say this. Wentworth was here at pains to restrict the scope of his words: 'How far can you stretch these words of her unkindly abusing and opposing herself ...? Can you apply them any further than I have applied them, that is to say that in that her Majesty called the parliament of purpose to prevent traiterous perils to her person ...?' He then went on to repeat more of the original speech, which though perhaps beyond the point at which he had been stopped, explained his anxieties about the frustration of Parliament's efforts to safeguard the Queen's life.[17] Neale did not include Wentworth's answer defining the Queen's abuse of her people in his account, yet it it is perhaps an important clue to understanding why Wentworth's anger and frustration boiled over.[18]

Doubt remains, therefore, as to where the main concern lay. There are fine phrases about the necessity to talk of 'God's glory', and even a notion that those who brought messages preventing progress therein should be 'hanged'. It cannot really be argued, however, that there was an obvious preoccupation with it. Indeed religion almost appears to be occupying a subordinate role. The bishops, said Wentworth, declared themselves hostile to an active Commons participation in the legislative regulation of the Church in 1571, and there was a chance, then, that they had been responsible for the suppression of discussion again in 1572. What had happened then? The main business, for which everyone had been called by the Queen, was frustrated by none other than the Queen herself! Neale did, indeed, reflect an uncertainty about Wentworth's motivation at this point, namely whether religion or the succession – or the Queen's safety in the absence of a known order of succession – inspired Wentworth's speech, though as usual it is seen as part of what would have been a 'campaign' organised by Puritan extremists.[19]

Wentworth chose to suffer punishment, not for unequivocally urging the discussion of religious matters in defiance of the Queen, though he regretted the lack of progress here, but for disagreeing with her on an issue which had been cleared for discussion. It was here that he would not be silenced, and here that he exercised his free speech. He did so because he believed passionately that members of Parliament were charged with the task of defending Queen and country. They should do so against manifest error, even on the part of the Queen herself. Wentworth most obviously and dramatically chose to go into battle on the question of the Queen's safety and the closely-related question of secrecy of debate. Much of the speech is a eulogistic description of Parliament's function as a body of last resort for the correction of ills by means of consultation and lawmaking. It was also a complaint that confusion, and even abuse, had been generated by the Queen to the point of endangering lives.

Wentworth's questions about liberties in 1587 survive in two versions.[20] An immediate problem is that the two lists contain different numbers of questions, and the areas covered by them are not wholly identical, or arranged in the same order. These differences make it hard to decide which, if any, are the authentic Wentworth elements. So it is important to analyse their meaning, or, more specifically, to decide if either of the sets of questions shows a watertight, revolutionary definition of free speech in the way which Neale believed was Wentworth's singular achievement.[21]

Peter Wentworth revisited

The Lansdowne list is pre-eminently concerned with two points, the first of them being the view that 'Parliament' played an indispensable part in the protection of the prince and state, that its laws were repealable only by itself, and that free speech – undefined – was customarily granted to its members 'by law'. The *usefulness* of free speech and the need to protect it (unless it spilled over into traitorous talk) from attacks by 'messages', or by leaking information about proceedings 'unto the prince', appear to be the second main concern. In these respects Wentworth says no more than had been said before, and many of the 1587 questions are echoes of 1576. Two questions, however, *could* be more wide-ranging and thrusting. One of them asks: 'Whether this be a place to receive supplications of the greifs and sores of the commonwealth, and either that we should be humble suitors unto the Queen her majesty for relief, or else to relieve them here as the case requireth' (Number 6). As it stands, this may be seen as a simple statement of the historical picture, and it makes the distinction between petitioning and proceeding by bill which Elizabeth was thought to have favoured. It is also the item which approximates most closely to the first one in the other version: 'Whether this Council be not a place for any member of the same here assembled, freely and without controlment of any person or danger of laws, by bill or speech to utter any of the griefs of this commonwealth whatsoever touching the service of God, the safety of the prince and this noble realm.' It could be that this was where Wentworth's revolutionary distillation was most apparent. This can only be true, however, if the words 'by bill or speech' were interpreted as widely as possible, that is to say, so that they gave the *member* the option of deciding by which avenue to proceed. If, however, Wentworth is simply noting that there are different procedures when dealing with the problem of griefs, then his statement again becomes unexceptionable, because descriptive.

The other question (Number 5) asks whether it is against the law (presumably of privilege) for the Queen or the Privy Council to send for a member during the session and to blame or punish him 'for any speech used in this place, except it be for traitorous words'. These words may be seen as wide probing of the limits of free speech, because they could mean that Wentworth argued that *anything* other

135

than traitorous words should be allowed. On the other hand, his concern could equally be merely to establish that members should feel no inhibitions when speaking on authorised topics. There is no clear indication that Wentworth's thought at this point was concerned specifically with range and scope, rather than trying to ensure that authorised debate be conducted without fear of recrimination. Uncertainty remains, therefore, and the other seven questions in the D'Ewes version are echoed in Lansdowne and are concerned with a description of Parliament's sovereign lawmaking role and the benefits of free speech (again undefined) in fulfilling it.[22]

Wentworth's action in 1587 has long been associated with the introduction of Cope's Bill and Book; and the parliamentary timetable certainly seems to bear this out. On 27 February Cope produced his documents before the House, though intervention by the Speaker and others meant that the decision to read the bill was frustrated. Two days later, Wentworth made his short speech in which he urged the Speaker to put to the House his questions on 'free speech and consultation'. Members might thus be guided and instructed in how far they 'may proceed ... being fearful and loth to give or offer any offence to her Majesty'. The questions, as we know, were 'pocketed up' by the Speaker, and Wentworth was in the Tower by the afternoon. The following day a handful of members who had spoken in favour of Cope's Bill were also sent to the Tower, and Burghley was writing to James VI's ambassador to say that Job Throckmorton was to be detained for a speech made in Parliament.[23]

Wentworth, however, was not among those recorded as speaking in favour of Cope's proposals, and while this does not prove that he did not speak, or that his motivation was other than religious, it does mean that we have to be cautious about explaining the appearance of the questions. These do not give an unambiguous indication of what influenced Wentworth here, and in that respect they resemble his intervention in 1576. It is important to remember what was happening in Parliament in the last days of February 1587, because there were other important matters on the agenda. On 22 February Hatton had stressed the great dangers to England from the foreign situation, and Mildmay had explained the consequent need for a subsidy. On the following day Throckmorton, speaking on this 'authorised' topic, emphasised the desirability of Elizabeth's taking the sovereignty of the Netherlands and launched a strong personal attack on both the

Spanish king and James VI. A diarist noted that he had 'spoken sharply' of princes and been rebuked by Hatton as a result.[24] Two days later Hatton, alone or prompted from other quarters, moved that Throckmorton be admonished because he had spoken 'sharply of princes and laid indignities on them. The reverence to princes is due by God .... We should use great regard of princes in free speech.' By 27 February (or perhaps the following day) the committee looking into the question of granting Elizabeth money in addition to the subsidy – and counting Throckmorton among its members – was moving in favour of using the benevolence to pressurise Elizabeth into accepting the sovereignty, and Hatton himself was willing, apparently, to agree to this.[25]

Irrespective of what Cope attempted on 27 February, therefore, we may imagine that Elizabeth was not happy about what was happening in the Commons, or among her councillors there. Throckmorton's offence was particularly acute from her point of view. Hatton had at least rebuked Throckmorton on her behalf for his intemperate language, though it may not have been wise to do so by a positive invocation of the ultimate limitations of free speech. Throckmorton was not cowed though, for he produced another long speech on 27 February after Cope's attempts to have his bill adopted. Like Lewknor and others who spoke in apparent support of Cope by extolling the virtues of a well-qualified ministry, Throckmorton emphasised the shortcomings of a 'dumb ministry', and this was presumably why Neale saw the speech as part of the Presbyterian campaign which Cope hoped to launch. Throckmorton did, however, range more widely than this. For one thing, he had prefaced the substantial part of his oration with the complaint that members were generally made aware that 'reformation of religion and *the establishment of the succession*' were not to be discussed.[26] If those in high places dealt with these matters properly, he said, there would be no need for others to do so. He did not say why he supported Cope's proposals for the Church (though we may wonder why not), but he did declare his fulsome support for a learned ministry, aligning himself most clearly with the mainstream support for Church reform which was to go on once Cope's action had been stopped. This was again undoubtedly a speech for the succession, whatever else it was. The grey heads of Councillors should not remain silent, said Throckmorton. Although Mary had suffered the just penalty at last, it was still necessary 'to settle the Crown to the bliss of posterity'. Mary was described as 'that Guisian imp', to add to remarks about 'that young imp' (James VI) which, only days earlier, had brought Hatton down on his neck. To the Queen, Throckmorton must have seemed irrepressible, and he was imprisoned. Wentworth himself witnessed a situation where another member, concerned about the welfare of the realm, had been incarcerated. He had already shown in 1576 how concerned he was about the vulnerability of members who demonstrated their concern for the Queen's safety. It may be that on this occasion he was impelled to raise similar questions about privilege in the context of related urgent matters.[27]

There remains no direct evidence that Wentworth's arrest in 1587 was for speaking on Cope's behalf, or for seeking to interpret free speech so widely as to make Parliament a safe place for Cope to work in. In 1593, when Wentworth again became involved in the troubled waters of the succession issue, James Morice advised caution, reminding him of his imprisonment. 'You and others were committed to the Tower for conference in matters of religion ....' This has been taken as evidence that Wentworth's activities in 1587 were connected with Cope's moves, but Morice was advising Wentworth of the folly of being discovered talking of state matters outside Parliament, and comparison of 1587 and 1593 holds good on that score.[28] Wentworth needed to beware of the danger of falling technically foul of the rules. The arrests of Lewknor and others who had supported Cope were not avowedly undertaken for what had been said in Parliament, but on the *technicality* that they had spoken about business outside the House, which was forbidden. It is not implausible, then, that Wentworth was, as Morice said, arrested for conferring about religion in 1587, but that by doing so he had given the Queen the opportunity to stifle his unwelcome intervention on the sensitive matter of the succession, raised on the pretext that the safety of the realm was what Parliament had been called to give advice on. In so far as Morice's account is relevant to a reconstruction of the events of 1587 it does not necessarily tell us anything about Wentworth's motivation inside Parliament. It gives a reason for Wentworth's arrest, though it does not explain it.[29]

MEMBERS OF THE COMMONS AND FREE SPEECH

We still have to ask whether Wentworth tried to claim that Parliament had a right to talk about issues, despite what the Queen said, and that this right existed by virtue of special powers possessed by its constituent parts. It is interesting to note that the great speech of 1576 came out of the blue, almost at the beginning of the session and without being connected apparently to any religious issue under discussion at the time. It was not something which had been provoked by an immediate religious repulse from the Supreme Governor. It was not a riposte of the Puritan trying to launch a campaign, unless it is one we know nothing of. The speech bears the hallmark of Wentworth's frustrated mind, pent up for three years or more. He spoke of events in the 1572 parliament. He had been deeply affected by what he had seen then, and in 1576 his indignation erupted. His concern was to remedy the ills of the realm, and he believed this was the purpose of parliamentary meetings. The Lord Keeper said so in so many words at the start of a new parliament. The wants and excesses of the realm were to be supplied and reformed, and this was to be done by attention to the law. In a way what Wentworth says about Parliament is tautology, though it is sometimes gloriously phrased. He says, emotionally, what everyone knew to be true, though what is not clear is how far he imagined the truth could, or should, be pushed. It is possible that Wentworth may have simply asked quite innocently for definition of these vague areas, so as to know what could be safely said in future. He makes this point explicitly, though perhaps disingenuously, in 1587 in a speech usually though to have been written by him, but which was supposed to have been delivered by another member in his support. This suggestion is supported at face value, at least, by his reference in 1576 to the great doubts many had had when they stood up to speak in 1572 about Mary Stuart and the Duke of Norfolk.[30]

The suggestion is that Wentworth was talking about the freedom to speak without harassment. He devoted much attention to rumours and messages. He did not unambiguously demand the freedom to speak on any matter he chose, but he asked to be able to speak freely on matters put before him. If this was so, perhaps he should not have made so much trouble. He should have heeded Elizabeth's word when she withdrew her consent for further discussion. This objection can only be met in the context of the supreme urgency attached to consideration of the realm's safety, one of the main, and regularly declared, purposes of parliamentary gatherings. Wentworth did not intend to construe free speech in an extravagant and widely drawn sense. He simply wanted to stick to the agenda as Elizabeth had first set it out. If the foregoing argument is correct, then the need to assume a fundamental change in Wentworth's career, as Neale does, disappears.[31]

If the succession was Wentworth's major preoccupation, then it is important to stress that he was not unique. Everyone wanted an answer to the problem. As we know, the Commons drafted a petition in 1566 asking the Queen to determine who would succeed her. Subsequent developments led to the further request for a guarantee of 'our accustomed lawful liberties'. At one point at least then, free speech was regarded as a matter of law, as Wentworth himself was later keen to stress.[32]

In 1572 the other elements which prefigured Wentworth's contribution appeared in the debates over Mary Stuart. Thomas Norton had already asserted the necessity of keeping speech 'free of unjust slanders and undeserved reproaches' in 1571, because he felt he had been described as being 'doubly disposed' and representing an 'especial party' when he attacked Mary Stuart in the debate on the treason bill.[33] It was Mary Stuart who was again the occasion for more agitation in 1572, when a speech by Robert Snagge was apparently misreported to the Lords. 'I desired at the same time', said Snagge commenting on the speech which had caused the trouble, 'I might be heard with indifferent ears and conceived with indifferent judgment.' He commented further that he had feared he would be misreported by sinister parties, and Wentworth himself objected to tale-tellers at this point. Speaker Bell also condemned the situation. It was Christopher Yelverton, however, a future Speaker himself, who upheld the secrecy of debate, if only, he said, because 'zeal' could sometimes lead members to be indiscreet in their speeches. Such indiscretions, if reported, could cause dissension between the Queen, the nobility and us, 'which representeth the commonalty'. Unless free speech were allowed, he said, members would respond to their anxiety about being reported by falling silent, 'and then bad laws are to be looked for'. Fleetwood, another member who, like Norton, was closely connected to official circles, claimed that those who tried to cause trouble by reporting speeches were evil Papists, and their offence, he said, was tantamount to treason. Even if Wentworth was primarily concerned with the need to be able to pursue *religious* issues freely in the House, we have to acknowledge that others shared his resentment.[34] The Speaker's announcement of Elizabeth's ban on religious bills on 22 May 1572 – the message to which Wentworth referred in his speech in 1576 – apparently caused private comment among members, though nothing was apparently said on the floor of the House about the threat to the Commons' liberty.[35]

Many of the ingredients of Wentworth's major speech are therefore apparent some time before it was delivered, and arguably some of the passion he brought to his subject was present too. In this sense it is still correct to see his contribution as a distillation of others' concerns. What is not so clear is whether he pushed the thought on to a revolutionary footing. There were other contributions in any case which must be taken into account, if only to see him in proper context. For example, the notes made in the parliament of 1586–87 by another member, Thomas Cromwell, can hardly be ignored, for they speak in terms which are every bit as extravagant, if imprecise, as Wentworth's own.[36] Cromwell's researches among the parliamentary records were meant to provide a justification for protesting about the continued detention of those members who had spoken in support of Cope, though they had, of course, fallen foul of the rule about discussion outside the House. The document which has survived shows how fertile the imagination of members could be. An act of Edward III, which declared there should be annual parliaments, served as the basis for as broad a concept of free speech as Wentworth may ever have supported. If, as the act said, parliaments were to hear grievances, then it must follow that it was 'lawful for every member of the House to open that which he conceiveth to be a grievance, and withal to offer that which he taketh to be a remedy, and also to consider and confer thereof'. Here the liberty is perhaps widely drawn, but also, as with Wentworth and his colleagues earlier, it was lawful, by which was meant that it was established by law and not merely 'justifiable' or 'reasonable'. After more precedents came the comment that freedom of speech was necessary for 'such as are to make laws, for of dumbness evil laws are always to be expected': thus Cromwell, thus Yelverton in 1572. Another case from Henry VIII's reign (Strode) was generously interpreted: 'it seemeth to be lawful to prefer bills, to speak reason, and confer of matters to be commissioned or reasoned of in Parliament, and that no punishment should be for doing thereof'. In view of the arrest of some members in this session, supposedly for their participation in the debates on religion, there was just as much concern in the document for members who had thus been prevented from attending the House; but the preoccupation is clear. To function as it was meant to function, as the place where sores are healed, as Wentworth said, then all members should be free to attend and to speak. The word 'parliament' 'seemeth to be devised by the French words "parle" and "ment", which is "speak the mind" '. None of this is formulated in as precise terms as one might wish, but the drift of Cromwell's work came as close as Wentworth did to saying that there was no limit to what might be said. Whatever Wentworth was most concerned about, he was never a lone voice.[37]

NOTES

1 Graves, *Elizabethan Parliaments*, especially p. 46.

2 Neale, 'Peter Wentworth', p. 175.

3 Neale, 'Peter Wentworth', pp. 40–1.

4 *Procs.*, pp. 425–34; Neale, 'Peter Wentworth', pp. 44–5; Neale speaks of Wentworth's theories of privilege here, though it is not clear what was at issue, and whether it was the attack on the secrecy of proceedings which Gilbert's report to parties outside the House constituted, or the attack on being able to speak free of the fear of having words twisted by malicious reports. Neither of these *necessarily* relates to the central doctrine of the freedom to initiate each and every topic in the House, though they would no doubt have been considered useful adjuncts.

5 Neale, 'Peter Wentworth', p. 46.

6 Neale drew attention to the preoccupation with the succession: 'Peter Wentworth', p. 37.

7 *EP*, i.325; D'Ewes's editor printed the speech, though the MS journal merely refers to it, and speculates that it was Knollys's message about Mary Stuart, rather than a prohibition of religious discussion, which was the bone of contention; BL Harley MS 74, fos. 66–v.

8 Neale, 'Peter Wentworth', p. 43.

9 *Procs.*, pp. 426–9.

10 *EP*, i.321.

11 *EP*, i.321; *Procs.*, pp. 264, 417, 426–9.

12 *Procs.*, p. 427.

13 *Procs.*, p. 432; D'Ewes has no record of the message, which came on 22 May 1572, but says the instruction Wentworth referred to was not to deal

further in the matter of the Scottish Queen, recorded under 28 May 1572: D'Ewes, *Journals*, pp. 219, 238, 241; *EP*, i.302.

14 *Procs.*, p. 432.

15 *Procs.*, pp. 430, 431, 438.

16 *Procs.*, pp. 435–9.

17 *Procs.*, p. 438.

18 *EP*, i.326–9.

19 *EP*, i.329–30.

20 One is printed in D'Ewes, *Journals*, p. 411, though Neale believed that the other version (BL Lansdowne MS 105, fo. 182) was Wentworth's own ('Peter Wentworth', p. 49).

21 The list in D'Ewes has eight questions, Lansdowne's, ten. The fourth item of the D'Ewes list apparently corresponds with the eighth in the Lansdowne manuscript.

22 Numbers 5 and 6 in D'Ewes (concerning the Speaker's role in the interruption of speeches, and the closing of proceedings by rising from the chair unilaterally) find no obvious echoes in Lansdowne.

23 *EP*, ii.148–9, 152.

24 *EP*, ii.169–73.

25 *EP*, ii.179.

26 *EP*, ii.150–1, my italics.

27 *EP*, ii.172; see 110–11 for concern for the succession in his speech against Mary.

28 *EP*, ii.258–9; Neale, 'Peter Wentworth', pp. 50–1.

29 In 1924 at least, Neale acknowledged that 'the connexion of Wentworth with Cope and the other imprisoned members is not clear': 'Peter Wentworth', p. 52.

30 BL Harley MS 1877, fos. 55–7; *EP*, ii.156.

31 Neale, 'Peter Wentworth', p. 175.

32 *Procs.*, p. 156.

33 *Procs.*, pp. 180, 203.

34 *Procs.*, pp. 403–5.

35 *EP*, i.302, 305–7, 405.

36 *EP*, ii.164–5; Northants CRO, Finch Hatton MS 16, fos. 547, 547v, 548v.

37 *EP*, i.325; see also *EP*, ii.26–7 for concern about curtailment of religious discussion in 1584 and 'searching' of the records to find precedents for parliamentary involvement.

Chapter 8

Elizabeth's last parliament

The parliamentary session of 1601 has been seen as almost a triumphant finale to the reign. A dangerous clash with the Commons was avoided by acceding to their pressure to reform monopolies, and the latest threats to the Queen's authority withered away under the impact of her inspired statesmanship.[1] The supremacy in the Church, which had been upheld in the face of the Puritan challenge, was matched by a reaffirmed supremacy in the State which had survived one of its biggest threats. It is clear that to the end the Queen did not wish to appear to be 'constrained' by her subjects gathered in the Houses of Parliament, but the view that the collapse of the Presbyterian onslaught of the 1580s had removed Parliament's ability to 'challenge' the Queen on her own ground must be modified (see Chapter 5). Though the Elizabethan heritage of peace and Protestantism was still the vision, and the substantial reality, which all loyal Englishmen carried before them, the Commons were prepared to do what they could to pressurise the Queen to settle the great problem of the day. This was another case where the the monarch's role of responsible, caring mother to her people was debated, and even doubted. Those who spoke in the Commons often did so on the premise that they were competent to see what was wrong and to envisage remedies. The only element that could not be taken for granted, it seemed, was the co-operation of the Queen herself. In the past the merely authoritarian standpoint which shaped her reaction to Parliament's initiatives had meant a negative outcome. On this occasion her response was more positive, though some attempt was made to avoid conceding that parliamentary pressure had produced it.

Parliament assembled on 27 October 1601 and it was dissolved nearly eight weeks later on 19 December. The opening brief given to the Houses by the Lord Keeper, Egerton, followed expected lines. Dangers from Rome and Spain meant that money was needed, and it was hoped to complete the session before Christmas. Perhaps it was not surprising, then, that he advised against making new laws, though the Houses were told to spend time reviewing existing ones.[2] Cecil later repeated the essence of this message in the Commons in response to complaints that many of the members had been unable to hear it at the bar of the Lords, having been shut out by an over-zealous usher. Somewhat paradoxically, however, the Lord Keeper's speech had contained an unusually specific suggestion for the Houses' attention, namely the problem of what he referred to as 'pettyfoggers and vipers of the commonwealth', those solicitors who were believed to be responsible for drumming up business for them-selves by means of encouraging dissension between men. It seems that an age-old concern about the legal profession had reached new heights, and that this had been sparked off by a noticeable increase in the amount of litigation being handled by the courts, though, ironi-cally, this may have passed its peak.[3] The degree of litigation in society was seen as a measure of its potential for lawlessness and instability. Indeed, a number of bills on the subject had appeared before this last session of the reign. Egerton's suggestion was fol-lowed up by the young parliamentary diarist Hayward Townshend, who later introduced a bill on the subject, citing the Lord Keeper's speech as his warrant. The concern in high places was thus as ever focused on the need to avoid invasion, the threat of 'tyrannical servi-tude' from abroad, and internal dissension; and the overriding needs for peace, concord, unity and the avoidance of strife were themselves significant elements in the picture which emerged in this session in the debates over monopolies.[4]

It goes without saying, however, that these did not wholly occupy Parliament's attention in 1601. Hayward Townshend's journal is a perfect illustration of the balance which usually existed in the Lower House between a single important issue like monopolies, and the continuing efforts which were expended in exercising a watching brief over the state of the law. Well over a hundred bills were given at least one reading, twenty-nine of them became acts, and another eight, covering a wide range of topics, passed both Houses but were refused the royal assent.[5] Much of what had happened here con-formed to the Queen's view of legitimate parliamentary activity and was therefore unexceptional, even if she was moved by various con-siderations to veto some. The session was, however, by no means free of a range of measures whose mere existence was a challenge to her claim to limit, if not to frame precisely, the parliamentary agenda.[6]

In the religious sphere alone, bills to limit activity on the sabbath and to control pluralities in the Church made defiant reappearances from earlier sessions.[7] They may have become paler, or distinctly different versions of their earlier incarnations, and they perhaps inevitably failed to make real headway; but it does not look as though the absence of a strong and vigorous so-called 'Puritan opposition' provides the explanation. Whatever the precise nature of religious discontent in earlier parliaments, there had been little statutory suc-cess. By this stage there was nothing to be lost by making prudent changes to earlier measures in the faint hope that even Elizabeth might at last see some virtue in them. The Pluralities Bill *was* argu-ably mauled by Whitgift's supporters, but its continued existence, threatening the Church with parliamentary control despite Convoca-tion's action on pluralities in 1597, was anathema to the Queen and ensured that she reacted in her accustomed way.

The Exchequer Bill was another defiant repeat appearance. The issue was first raised in 1571 by Robert Bell and it emerged in 1589 as a bill, presented to the House by Sir Edward Hoby. This was apparently an independent gesture as Hoby complained that he had been rebuked for his action by a 'great personage'.[8] On that occasion, as indeed now in 1601, the Exchequer official (other than the Chancellor himself) who was most closely involved, and who was also a member of the House, was consulted on all the relevant stages of the matter, and the bill sailed through both Houses. In 1601 the intention was to incorpo-rate into statute the orders taken by Elizabeth in 1589 after quashing the bill. Clearly the problem had not been resolved. On 18 November Bacon was able to report that the Queen's interests had been carefully preserved. 'The bill is both public and private', he said, 'public, be-cause it is to do good unto the subject, and private, because it doth no injustice to the particular office.' Here was an illuminating indication of the way the parliamentary mind was working in the midst of the developing monopolies question. In this instance, Parliament had been the forum for a resolution of potentially conflicting interests, including the royal preserve of the prerogative itself and with the co-operation of the the Queen's own men. A solution had emerged and it was only the Queen herself who prevented its realisation.[9]

MONOPOLIES

It is the question of monopolies, however, which has long excited observers and historians of the parliamentary scene. As far as we can tell, the Lords never became directly involved, but the issue provided one of the most arresting examples of how the Commons could air a grievance and show enormous strength of feeling against the monarch's known sensitivity about an aspect of her prerogative power. The term 'monopoly' is used to describe a range of privileges granted to individuals by the monarch, but those relating to trade and manu-facturing are probably the best known. They were not new in 1601, but the issue had arguably become more serious simply because the worst aspects of monopolies had become well recognised. As long ago as 1571 Robert Bell had drawn attention to the potential dangers of the situation.[10] The crux of the matter was that monopolies in one form or another presented the spectacle of politically sanctioned privileges for the individual over the community, simply by virtue of conferring powers of monopolistic activities in specified fields of commerce and industry. Supposedly granted to protect these indi-viduals against loss in risky new ventures which could, and ought to be of benefit to society at large, some of them were plainly being abused in a number of ways. It is clear now that the pressure which built up in the House over monopolies in 1601 would be hard to resist, especially as failure to tackle the problem could seem callous, or reveal a complacency about the consequences of a practice which had been condemned strongly enough in the 1597–98 parliament. In 1601, the issue was first raised on the floor of the House on 4 November, and even after the resolution of the matter at the end of the month it seems monopolies coloured members' perceptions of other issues. In 1597 it had been decided to petition the Queen about the matter, and Robert Wingfield, one of the activists then, emerged at the forefront again in 1601.[11] It was he who drew attention to the failure of the Queen's earlier promise that action would be taken to subject the operation of the patents 'to the true touchstone of the law'. Limiting the extavagances of monopolies by process of law was to be the solution as it finally emerged in 1601 after much discussion and manoeuvring. After Parliament ended in 1598, Elizabeth had not seen fit to follow through her promise. She was obviously keen in both sessions to avoid the formal emergence of either petition or bill, so the news that something was in the offing was enough to provoke one of her famous promises for action on the first occasion.[12] Members might have suspected, though they were not to know, that little would come of it, but it is hard to agree that the Commons in 1597 had been 'mild and proper, not to say supine' in opting for a petition, for their protests were clearly offensive to Elizabeth in themselves.[13]

Whatever the case in 1597, the action was not supine in 1601. Wingfield drew attention to the fact that the problem remained, and said graphically that 'the wound, Mr Speaker, is still bleeding'. Given the Elizabethans' predilection for using the physical body as a metaphor for the body politic, these words are significant, for they explain the full force of much of the concern expressed in the Commons in the course of the ensuing debates. Monopolies were seen by this time as comprehensively unacceptable, attracting a catalogue of complaints, economic, social and political. They are evident in the speeches which Hayward Townshend recorded, and also from his account of a 'paper' shown him on 23 November by another member, possibly Wingfield, which listed the ways in which some of the monopolies were thought to be failing the litmus test of benefiting society at large.[14]

A whole range of goods such as vinegar, salt, wine, leather and tin were said to have deteriorated in quality as a result of the granting of monopolies of production. Pots, bottles and brushes had doubled, and trebled, in price. Steel, also at inflated prices, was of inferior quality because its content was 'mixed', and many workers who had been able to make a living from the production of tools with sharp edges had been reduced to beggary. Attention was also drawn to starch and glass products, which commonly used to be obtained from abroad. Licences had been granted for their production at home, and no foreign goods were to be allowed to compete. The rationale may have been to create employment in the realm, but it was claimed that these grants resulted in the unnecessary consumption of precious timber fuel, as well as often enhancing prices and reducing the Queen's income from customs previously levied on the imports. The practice of imprisoning ships' masters until they promised, by bond,

not to import foreign glass products was also a disincentive to ship-
ping, an important consideration from the point of view of encouraging shipbuilding for maritime defence.

One of the more interesting examples in the paper which Townshend was shown was the case of the playing-card monopoly, which
was to become a test case shortly after the ending of Parliament. It
was alleged that production was widespread before the grant and the
employment it generated was, therefore, considerable. Since the
grant, the price of cards had soared. The purchaser was now given no
choice other than to buy from one supplier and to buy, moreover,
sight unseen; for each pack was sealed and the customer was 'unable
to see what he bought and make choice of his liking'.[15]

While it could be argued that the various grants were undesirable
from an industrial and commercial point of view, members were
concerned with other issues in their speeches, either in the House
itself or its committee. They displayed their hostility to the ways the
monopoly grants were enforced, and to the threats to good order and
what we may call 'proper process' that this entailed. They spoke with
the authority of local representatives well versed in what was happening in their own areas. The monopolists, or more often their deputies
or 'substitutes', were regarded by some as scoundrels, who could not
be trusted to behave appropriately. Some thought their irregularities
could easily be prevented. Mr Dyott, the Recorder for Tamworth in
Staffordshire, offered a solution at an early stage:

> there be many commodities ... which being public for the benefit of
> every particular subject are monopolised ... only for the good and
> private gain of one man. To remedy the abuses of those kind of
> patents which are granted for a good intent by her Majesty, I am, Mr
> Speaker, to offer ... an act against patents purporting particular power
> to be given to sundry patentees.

Another member then apparently offered a much more pithy bill
which simply set out the common law position *vis-à-vis* monopolies,
presumably allowing the grants – and therefore, by extension, this
aspect of the royal prerogative – to be subject to testing in the courts
on a statutory basis.[16]

Dyott's approach avowedly involved no wholesale attack on the
Queen's powers to grant monopolies, and he recognised that grants
were made in order to serve the common good. This was a point later
endorsed by Francis Bacon, who explained that some of the grants

had recently been subjected to trial at common law. If the judges discovered the grant to be 'good and beneficial for the commonwealth they will allow it, otherwise disallow it'. Drastic action *had* been taken in a number of cases, therefore, and the Commons committee, considering how best to proceed, learned that the salt monopolist had been instructed to reduce prices which had apparently risen tenfold or more. There was much anxiety because bad practices persisted in other cases, and the call was obviously for a wholesale and concerted policy. Abuse of monopoly powers, rather than the monopolies themselves, was the problem, though the approach through a statutory intrusion into the forbidden territory of the prerogative itself, even if only to uphold the original object of royal grants, was not likely to gain Elizabeth's sympathy. Though there was continuing concern in the House about whether to proceed by bill, or to petition Elizabeth to remedy the grievance, members' commitment to achieving a remedy did not diminish, and their tongues were not silenced.

Mr Spicer of Warwick remains one of the most eloquent critics. His attack on the monopolist's officers he had encountered – men he tellingly described as 'ill-disposed and evil members of the commonwealth' – gives us a clear insight into concerns expressed and hinted at by others. He was especially affronted that one such officer he had encountered was a recusant, obstinate and barely loyal to the Queen. The allegation of a Catholic presence in this field might have had a profound effect when members were still fearful of threats to Protestant England, but it was closely associated with Spicer's major anxiety about how the situation had got out of hand. How was it that such a man had been able to break through procedures intended to control monopolies and make them consistent with good order and reasonableness? The agent, said Spicer, had come to Warwick to enforce his master's sole right of sale of the particular product. Other vendors would have to cease their activities and find other livelihoods. While the grant *itself* specified that a period of six months' grace should be allowed for them to do so, they had, in fact, been shut down within two months. Those accused of infringing the grant were also supposed to be brought before Justices of the Peace, where bonds should be taken for their good behaviour pending a determination of their case before the Exchequer. This too was being ignored, and agents were taking bonds themselves, and 'so by usurpation retaineth power ... both to kill and save'. Spicer expressed outrage and desperation that the usual safeguards were being flouted, and that unreasonable treatment was being meted out to others. A similar sort of problem seemed to be an odious feature of the playing-card monopoly, as outlined in Wingfield's notes on various grants. It was that infringers of the patent were threatened with imprisonment 'if they will not release themselves by a ransom of money'. It is hard to avoid the conclusion that members felt that the control of monopolies on the ground was being diverted away from safe hands, and that it was the Justices of the Peace who could, perhaps ought to, be an effective check on any excesses which might creep into their implementation. This, as we shall see, was an important point in view of later developments.[17]

Many ills were laid at the doors of patentees in 1601, then, and there is scarcely a note of sympathy for the monopolists recorded by the diarist Hayward Townshend. Cecil himself, as well as Raleigh, are the obvious exceptions to this, though they scarcely launched a defiant counter-attack. In some parts of the realm, moreover, it was claimed that control of most of the main commodities was in the hands of 'these bloodsuckers of the commonwealth'. An injury had been done to the commonwealth, and one member wondered how 'the good estate of that body [could] long remain' if it were left still bleeding and languishing? 'What shall become of us, from whom the fruits upon our own soil and the commodities of our own labour ... shall be taken away by warrant of supreme authority which the poor subject dares not gainsay?' Yet another member picked up this thread and detected a danger of disorder. Using the conventional corporal analogy, he said the subject was the foot and the Queen the head, and if we are not careful, 'the foot riseth against the head'.[18]

It was clear that a bill would be considered an assault of the prerogative, and many members therefore wanted a humble petition to be addressed to the Queen. The House had already been alerted to this problem when it had considered the Pluralities Bill, and Sergeant Harris pointed out that 'the last parliament may be a warning to us when the like bill was preferred by us, and the same not only rejected, but also her majesty commanded the Lord Keeper to tell us that she hoped we should not hereafter meddle in cases of this nature so nearly touching her prerogative royal'. But some members feared that a petition would produce nothing; this had been the strategy in 1597–98, and nothing had come of it. There was unease about trusting royal undertakings, therefore, and it was folly for Sir Thomas Fleming, the Solicitor-General, to claim that progress had been held up because of the Essex rebellion of February 1601. This was a transparent excuse for inaction, and someone pointed out there had been time enough *before* the Essex venture. It may be that Cecil and others had contemplated some action before Parliament assembled, but if so, it was late in the day, and there were contradictory signs as well. As late as 7 October 1601 the Privy Council was openly support-ing grants.[19] Royal promises were not guarantees of action, though making real headway by means of legislation, even if Elizabeth could be brought to assent to a bill passed through the Lords and Com-mons, was also a problem, for the basis of many monopolies was a dispensation from the operation of current legislation which would otherwise have rendered the monopolists' activity illegal. What was there to prevent the Crown from dispensing from any new law? This posed an insuperable obstacle for the Commons, and it also brought into sharp relief the gulf between the Queen and subject, even her leading subjects in Parliament. This persisted to the point when the Lord Keeper's secretary, who was a member of the House, articulated further misgiving on 27 November about whether the Queen's proc-lamation (which had by this stage been promised) would actually appear in time. The suggestion that the Queen's promise to act be recorded in paper or parchment because 'records remain long and will give a lively memory in ages to come' is hardly surprising, though it was treated frostily by Sir William Knollys, Elizabeth's Comptroller. In the last resort, of course, there was nothing the Commons could do to force the Queen's hand by *constitutional* means. In the end, it was the pressure of the Commons' wish itself, together with any measure of feeling outside, which must have allowed Cecil and oth-ers to convince the Queen that a graceful and majestic show of compassionate surrender was needed.[20]

Whether or not what happened in Parliament was 'concerted', and by whom, remains unknown;[21] but what carried profound political weight in the end was that no one apparently supported the practice with any vigour or conviction. Dr Bennett, Chancellor of York Dio-cese, expressed his strong aversion to the effects of the salt monopoly in his own constituency. He then turned his attack on Sir Walter Raleigh, who was himself a monopolitan. Raleigh, it is true, re-sponded with a vigorous defence of his operation of the Cornish tin monopoly in comparison with that of his predecessor. The tin-workers were now much better off, he said, because he paid them steady wages, despite the changing market prices of tin. In this stalwart defence of himself Raleigh may have sold the pass, however, for by showing that there was a way in which monopolies need not benefit the holders alone, he risked showing that he was one of the exceptions to the general rule. The attack on monopolies was to all intents and purposes not argued against.[22] Raleigh said, after all, that he would be content to surrender his licence if it were for the general good; and later, when Cecil came to announce the revocation of many grants, he simply commented that in one case the monopolitan, a good and worthy man, had not even had an opportunity to apply his grant, but that nothwithstanding this it would be annulled.[23]

In fact it became clear during the last week of November that Elizabeth had decided to take action herself. Cecil announced the proclamation on 25 November. Given the anxiety roused by this issue, members were presumably relieved and gratified that it had been resolved with some dignity on both sides, though there may have been speculation about what had happened to persuade the Queen to act. When the Speaker first broke the news in the House, he emphasised Elizabeth's constant care for her subjects' welfare, and stressed that she was anxious to protect them from all oppressions. While he reported her thanks for the Commons' care of those things that concerned her state, and consequently themselves, he said that the information about monopolies had been brought to her by her councillors, and by petitions delivered to her on her way to chapel and elsewhere. She would therefore issue instructions herself to resolve the matter: 'we can see now that the axe of her princely justice is put to the root of the tree'. Moreover, her goodness had 'prevented', that is anticipated, their own counsels and consultations. Cecil added that the matter had not proceeded from any particular course 'thought upon', but from 'private information of some particular persons', though he seems to have acknowledged that they had been emboldened by knowing what was going on in the House. He suspected that Commons business was becoming common knowledge, and he cautioned the House that 'whatsoever is subject to a public expectation cannot be good. Why, Parliament matters are ordinary matters in the streets.' His concern that politics was becoming popularised, and that this would lead to disorder, may have been a smokescreen to discrdedit what he saw as anti-monopoly propaganda. It is just as likely, however, that he was genuinely concerned about the damage the issue had done, or could do, to the regime's integrity: 'the world is apt to slander most especially the ministers of government'.[24]

On 30 November the Queen met a large delegation from the Commons led by the Speaker, and received their thanks for her action. When she replied in the so-called 'golden speech', she seems to have acknowledged that there had been a parliamentary role, because she claimed she had 'received knowledge' from them about the true state of affairs.[25] According to Townshend's rather dense account at this point, however, the Speaker seemed to deny this: 'we cannot say we have called and we have been heard, we have complained and we have been helped'.[26] This may have been part of a polite and diplomatic pretence, of course. Other members obviously believed some of the stronger speeches in the House had been reported to the Queen, and some were unrepentant about this, discounting any notion that apologies should be made.[27]

It can not be doubted that the mere fact of a debate on monopolies was an annoyance to Elizabeth, but in her speech to the members she grasped the opportunity to establish her own side of the story. No prince, she said, could love subjects more than she had always done. If she agreed to grant privileges to patentees it was because she had been told that they would serve the common good. She had clearly been deceived in this on some occasions. Thus the Queen tried to distance herself from the harmful effects of her own action. There could no going back after the history of warning and complaint: however it was dressed up, there was no escaping the fact that an embarrassing climbdown had been accomplished by the Commons which had funnelled widespread complaint and directed it to Elizabeth herself. Action would be taken by a Queen who cared and had always cared. This is apparent in all the accounts of this speech which survive, but there is a further problem. It arises from what has been called the 'leaden' version of this speech. This is the copy which Elizabeth probably agreed could serve as the offical account, and it was approved for publication a few days after the event itself. This account shows little of the style and panache of the other versions, which presumably represent the attempts of a number of those present to record what had actually been said. There is no compelling reason, of course, why the 'official' version should be a true account of what was said, perhaps extempore, on 30 November. If there was a version which Elizabeth was prepared to release as the historical record, it may be that she took the opportunity to adjust the emphasis of what had been said. The leaden version has one important element not present in the others. It is an insistence that it was her right to reward whomsoever she chose by means of her prerogative. If Elizabeth was prepared to publish her magnanimity to the world, in this version it looks as though she ensured that her prerogative position was also clearly stated.[28]

THE WIDER IMPLICATIONS

Finding the best way of dealing with monopolies was in a sense merely an aspect of the major political question involved, and Cecil understood this well enough. In the earlier stages of the discussion, he had said that two great matters were in question, the prince's power and the subject's freedom; and no more tender points had been handled in Parliament. He was in some difficulty, he said, as a servant of the Queen who was also an Englishman, but he concluded that 'I had rather all the patents burnt than that her Majesty should lose the hearts of so many subjects.' It was wrong that grants should take away the subject's birthright. The Secretary had to act as the Queen's spokesman to a House which had grown impatient for action and apt to suspect that it would not happen. In a later speech, Cecil was able to add to this conviction by commenting on how the grants had been executed throughout the country in the first place. According to Townshend's report, this had barely been raised before this moment. It had been mentioned in Wingfield's paper in connection with the playing-card monopoly, but no member is recorded as speaking about it.[29]

Cecil pointed out that:

> most of these patents have been supported by letters of assistance from her Majesty's privy council .... I do assure you that from henceforth there shall be no more granted .... But to whom do they [the monopolists' deputies] repair with these letters? To some out house, to some desolate widow, to some simple cottage or poor ignorant people who rather than they would be troubled and undo themselves ... will give anything in reason for these caterpillars' satisfaction.[30]

A letter of assistance was a general letter of command obtained by the patentee and addressed to all sheriffs, Justices of the Peace, mayors and other public officers; and it required them to assist the patentee in the enforcement of his privilege against encroachments. In theory at least, this involved the open and active association of governors of the realm with the acts of suppression to which Cecil had alluded. A Privy Council letter of 28 April 1601, for example, directed officers to prevent the sale of imported pottery by helping in arresting or searching of ships, warehouses, cellars, shops, rooms or any other place, and in seizing goods and arresting the persons involved.[31] It may be that these letters were an acute embarrassment to the regime. They were certainly mentioned in the proclamation which eventually announced sweeping action against monopolies. Again, the view announced there was that they were based on 'false suggestions' which Elizabeth said had been made to her in support of applications for grants.[32]

In the end it was possible to argue that, because the protest had been made in the form of a petition, the prerogative had not been directly confronted or tainted. The Commons, after all, were simply exercising their right to petition for redress of grievances, and Elizabeth herself had said that the Commons should handle commonwealth matters. We have seen throughout the reign that there were occasions when virtually the whole of the House – Councillors and all – were at one against the Queen, together with many of the Lords too, and yet she remained unmoved. The monopolies question appears to be of paramount importance. The challenge over monopolies has usually been seen as another issue which tested the resolve of the Queen to stand by her prerogative, but something larger than that had been at stake. There was more involved than the Queen simply trying to hold on to her freedom to finance and reward officers and favourites in a particular way so as to save unnecessary expenditure herself.[33]

The debate on monopolies and its immediate outcome seemed to have concentrated minds on the nature, and the integrity, of the regime itself. Another measure of the sensitivity of the members to matters of this sort emerged in later debates. In the course of a bill aimed at curtailing swearing, Edward Glascock, a young lawyer, appeared to launch a strong attack on Justices of the Peace. The view that Justices of the Peace could be corrupt and partial was no novelty, but that did not make it any the more acceptable to a House of Commons containing a large proportion of serving magistrates. To entrust the execution of more laws to these men, said Glascock, was folly, for they would do very little 'unless you offered them sacrifices'. They were 'basket justices' who responded to gifts of chickens, for example, rather than to notions of justice.

Glascock was not alone in his unfavourable opinions of some Justices, and what was perhaps especially galling was the view that fair trial before Justices could not be taken for granted. A bill, presumably officially inspired, came before the House and was designed to secure the better levying of the shilling recusancy fine as prescribed in the 1559 Act of Uniformity. It relied essentially on transferring the task of execution from churchwardens, ultimately disciplined by assize judges, into the hands of two Justices of the Peace who would hear and determine cases on the evidence of two witnesses. Some felt this was a poor alternative to the previous reliance on the Justices in the assize courts where a jury of 'peers' operated, where in other words a principle of Magna Carta itself was said to be in play. It was said Justices were men, and were therefore subject to the frailties of human nature. The worst of it was that this baseness might threaten the security of the peace itself. The free-born subject was likely to be punished, and the common subject, 'whose strength and quietness is the strength and quietness of us all', would come off worse than anyone else, because it was not conceivable that Justices would 'contest with as good a man as himself'. Though in a subsequent speech Glascock himself protested that he had only been talking of the corrupt minority of Justices, he was unable to stop himself adding further insults. This time he spoke of 'uncuircumsized' Justices – *nouveaux riches* – whose new status exposed them to the temptations of abusing newly acquired powers, and also of 'adultering' Justices, that is those of good birth, but who were poor. It was a 'ground infallible', he said, that a poor man should not be given authority for 'the sweet scent of riches and gains takes away and confoundeth the true taste of justice and equity'. Moreoever the corruption which arose from these Justices, said Glascock, was the direct responsibility of members of the House because they as Justices recommended them for the bench to the Lord Keeper through the Justices of the assize.[34]

It was not surprising that these messages from a number of members stirred angry reactions. As we have seen, it was often suggested, or at least implied, that the Justice of the Peace was a guarantee against the greed of petty officers and against the potential excesses of higher authority. When there was a fear of the Crown or its agents exceeding their powers the solution was often to suggest a system of controls which meant in practice that the locality would be given powers of check and veto. To suggest now that such men were careless in recruiting to the bench, and tolerant of corruption, was an assault on the political integrity of the men who governed England. At a time when the scourge of monopolies had been confronted, and when men like Spicer had envisaged the Justice exercising an effective check on their excesses, thoughts such as these ran counter to the notion that Parliament was about advancing the cause of peace and good order. The notion that the Justice of the Peace was not to be trusted with power was seen by Comptroller Knollys as a threat to the whole political order: 'I much marvel that men will or dare accuse Justices of Peace, ministers to her Majesty without whom the commonwealth cannot be. If this boldness go on they will accuse judges, and lastly the seat of justice itself.' These attacks must have presented a threat to the political confidence of many members. Some of them considered them to be dangerous and hurtful to the Queen's honour. It was felt they were dangerous and potentially seditious, because such sentiments were becoming public knowledge and would be seen as a 'general slanderous imputation' to Justices.[35]

On 17 December, at the fag end of Parliament, Sir Francis Hastings rose and returned to the attack on Glascock and the others. Hastings was here endorsing Elizabeth's reign as a whole, and the happy marriage of peace and Protestantism. 'The church and commonwealth are two twins which laugh and live together', he said, and he wanted to guarantee a proper place for the Justice of the Peace who served 'religiously, dutifully and carefully'. The threats from Rome and Spain meant that everyone should continue to be vigilant in order to preserve Elizabeth's happy government: 'security without providence is dangerous'. In the same cautious vein he concluded with what appears to be an acknowledgement that Glascock may have had some grounds for complaint, at least. Those in supreme authority, he said, should be careful that 'those which have inferior governments will do faithfully and that we may be ruled in obedience'.[36]

Though an element of introspection had crept into proceedings, it did not preclude further discussion of matters where Elizabeth's discharge of her duties to her subjects came under scrutiny. A bill against the merchandising of iron ordnance appeared for its second reading on Tuesday, 8 December. It subsequently gathered the support of at least one Councillor in the House, though presumably its origins were unofficial, since it was obvious that it threatened the Queen's prerogative powers to grant patents to export cannon and other armaments. In the first place it is surprising that the measure was allowed into the House at all, for in 1593 someone had wanted to produce a similar bill, whereupon Elizabeth had written to Sir John Fortescue forbidding 'any such bill to be read. Mr Speaker acquainted the party delivering in the bill herewithal.'[37] In 1601, however, no such action appears to have been taken. There seems, however, to have been a widely recognised need for control. It was stressed that the trade was undesirable because foreigners were buying cannon of one bore, only to rebore them to a larger gauge, thereby deriving much needed further supplies of iron. So valuable was this that they now refused to import *any* English produce unless each ship carried a quantity of iron ordnance in the load. Elizabeth, it was claimed, was also receiving about £3,000 a year from the trade in customs duties. Arms were actually being supplied to confederates of our Spanish enemy; cutting off the supply would reduce Spain's strength and in seven years 'we might have him where we would'. It seemed strange that Spain was allegedly prohibiting the export of its horses, while we were arming 'our own enemies against ourselves'. Sir Walter Raleigh shared the view that Spain was now nearly matching the English in strength by virtue of English ordnance exports, and argued that possible diplomatic shifts betwen France, the Netherlands and Spain could well leave England weakened and isolated.[38]

Cecil had stressed the dangers from Spain at the start of this parliament, and here they became specifically involved with the Queen's profit and prerogative. Burghley's nephew Sir Edward Hoby indeed expressed concern that allowing the measure to go on would appear to be ungracious, in view of the Queen's recent action on monopolies. Another speaker then lamented that at that rate no progress could be made on many important matters because 'great or weighty' matters often came up against the objection that the Queen's prerogative was involved: 'and so we that come here to do our countries good bereave them of that good help we may justly administer'. Even Secretary Herbert agreed that action was necessary, though he naturally urged the House to petition the Queen. His idea was to appeal to the Queen's better judgement on the matter, a cautious suggestion not attracting universal support in the House. There were those who wanted to press on with the bill, even at the expense of shelving discussion of private bills, so as to avoid being left short of time. Another member pointed out that petitioning the Queen would mean that there would be no further statutory support for the inadequate law of Henry VIII, which, he said, offered insufficient penalties against offenders. Having heard these contrary opinions, the House committed the bill, despite Cecil's evident unease. Though a new bill emerged and was passed, nothing further came of it. In the course of all this it looks as though the Speaker and Comptroller Knollys in particular had been unhappy about giving free rein to a matter which would doubtless attract the Queen's hostility, and the Speaker may have gone against the wishes of the House in trying to deny reading the bill.[39] He also apparently 'forgot' to mention the matter in his address to Elizabeth during the closing proceedings, even though he had been asked to do so.[40]

This bill, thought necessary by many in the interests of national safety and 'to do our countries good', had attracted wide support; but Knollys was only stating the obvious when he told members that 'we must note that her self and her prerogative will not be forced'. Elizabeth probably intervened to stop further progress, not only on the Commons bill, but also on one with sharper teeth, which the Upper House itself had launched, apparently with some enthusiasm. The existence of a widespread inclination in both Houses to act on this subject manifests some disquiet among Elizabeth's advisers and governors about the safety of the Protestant state. As with monopolies, the Queen's sensitiveness about her prerogative had been ignored by the very existence of these bills, because members of the Lords and Commons felt she was not doing enough. The story of the Ordnance Bill of 1601 is of considerable importance because it suggests mistrust and lack of confidence in the Queen as the guardian of her subjects' safety which she had trailed as the hallmark of her reign.[41]

Feelings against monopolies had been strong, and could appear on other occasions. The problem appeared yet again on a personal level in a bill for the denization of a number of named individuals, including a certain Ralph Questor, brough into the House on 14 December. Apart from a difficulty over the appropriateness of denization for Questor, who did not technically qualify as neither parent was English, it was argued that his motivation was unworthy. He wanted to become English, it was said, simply to avoid paying the double subsidy which, as an alien, he was now required to do. More than this, he was said to be an 'engrosser' of fish. So once again the ugly spectre of monopolistic activities raised its head in the House. Both Raleigh and Cecil spoke on his behalf, and the House heard that he had long been a resident, and that there was not an 'honester man in England'. Cecil could not pronounce definitely on whether Questor was a monopolist of fish, though he declared that 'if I knew he were, I should hate him as I do monopolies'.[42]

It is hardly surprising that after a lifetime's practice Elizabeth was not able to let her hold on the prerogative slip for one moment, and she was never able, from succession to monopolies, to compromise what she saw as her own private position for the sake of her public duty. As in other instances, her difficulty in Parliament had not arisen from the irresponsible or extreme activities of a small band of zealous members, and there were occasions when, given the chance, the Lords were prepared to align themselves with the Commons on issues already ruled out of bounds. The failure on the Queen's part to be more positive about monopolies after the previous parliamentary session meant that when financial pressures drove her to summon the assembly again she was exposed to a powerful head of steam. Spicer's contribution to the debate remains one of the most telling, because it exposed some of the consequences of her defensive stand-point at a time when one of her favourite favourites had ridden through the streets of London in open revolt, and Spanish troops had walked the streets of Kinsale. Cecil knew very well the dangers of continuing to use the resources of the Tudor state, including the Justices themselves, to prop up monopolies which were not properly policed, and his avowed concern about losing the loyalty of the subject cannot lightly be dismissed. The attacks on Justices of the Peace which arose in other discussions in the House were not easily accommodated by the psychology of these governors of England, and members had to reassure themselves that Justices were indeed the pillar of the establishment.

It is hard to see how the Queen can have been anything but troubled by what had happened. The notion that, compared with earlier parliaments, this session was less vexacious[43] derives in part from a comparison of the notes for Lord Keeper Egerton's speech on 19 December and the reports of what was actually said on the occasion. These, it has been argued, show emphatically that Elizabeth was 'very far from considering the parliament of 1601 the most intransigent of her reign'.[44] There is a difference in the severity with which the encroachments on state matters are mentioned. In the notes, some 'few' members were said to have acted with more zeal than judgement, while the speech admitted that they had acted dutifully and had 'but *obiter*' touched the prerogative.[45] We do not know why this change occurred, or even if Egerton's working notes had been drafted on instruction from the Queen, which she then told him to modify on the occasion itself. The change may simply have been the result of the emollient ceremonial atmosphere of the closing procedures. Even if the Queen's hand had been at work here, it is not clear that the words signify a more clement view of events. It was not easy in this case to adopt the line so often used in the past, namely that trouble was the work of a misguided minority. The point being made was still that the prerogative must be inviolable, but faced with such a united front on monopolies even Elizabeth may have decided that graciousness rather than a lashing tongue was called for. Interestingly enough, the speech which she herself then delivered was devoted almost entirely to a lengthy analysis of the threats, internal, and from abroad, which she and the state had faced during her realm. The matter of monopolies was not specifically mentioned.[46]

NOTES

1 *EP*, ii.385; but see Guy, *Tudor England*, pp. 399–402.

2 See Russell, 'The nature of a parliament,' pp. 144–5; Graves, *Elizabethan Parliaments*, pp. 63–5.

3 Brooks, *Pettyfoggers and Vipers*, especially pp. 76–8, 136–8.

4 BL Stowe MS 362, fos. 62–v, 67–8v, 89–v, 94, 115v.

5 BL Stowe MS 362, fos. 262–70v; *EP*, ii.427.

6 *EP*, ii.427.

7 *EP*, ii.406–10.

8 *EP*, ii.207–8.

9 BL Stowe MS 362, fos. 116–17; D'Ewes, *Journals*, pp. 647, 684–5.

10 See Chapter 3; a bill had appeared in 1559, though nothing more is known about it, and in the early 1570s, possibly prompted by Bell's

intervention, a scheme of monopoly reform was envisaged, though by whom is not known: *PE*, p. 280.

11   *EP*, ii.353.

12   *EP*, ii.354–5.

13   BL Stowe MS 362, fos. 130v–1.

14   BL Stowe MS 362, fos. 138–9v.

15   BL Stowe MS 362, fos. 138v–9.

16   BL Stowe MS 362, fo. 117.

17   BL Stowe MS 362, fos. 125–7, 127–8, 138v–9.

18   BL Stowe MS 362, fos. 130–v.

19   Russell, 'English parliaments', p. 199; *APC* 1601–04, p. 237: see also *APC* 1600–01, pp. 274–5, 300–1.

20   BL Stowe MS 362, fos. 111–v, 136, 162–3.

21   *EP*, ii.381.

22   See *EP*, ii.378 for proponents of the softer approach, though the need for action was not in doubt.

23   BL Stowe MS 362, fos. 128–v, 131–2.

24   BL Stowe MS 362, fos. 149–50v, 151–3v; *EP*, ii.386.

25   B L Stowe MS 362, fo. 170.

26   BL Stowe MS 362, fos. 168–v.

27   BL Stowe MS 362, fos. 154v–5.

28   *EP*, ii.392; PRO SP 12/283/48.

29   BL Stowe MS 362, fos. 138v–9, 140v–1v.

30   BL Stowe 362, fos. 150v–4.

31   *APC* 1600–01, pp. 300–1.

32   Hughes and Larkin (eds.), *Tudor Royal Proclamations*, iii.235–8.

33   *EP*, ii.437.

34   BL Stowe MS 362, fos. 173–4v, 182–3v, 221–v, 250–2.

35   BL Stowe MS 362, fos. 180–v, 183, 184v–6.

36   BL Stowe MS 362, fos. 253v–4.

37   BL Cotton MS Titus Fii, fos. 62v–3.

38   BL Stowe MS 362, fos. 202v–6v.

39   D'Ewes, *Journals*, p. 677.

Elizabeth's parliaments

40 *EP*, ii.421–2; BL Stowe MS 362, fos. 258–v.

41 *EP*, ii.422.

42 BL Stowe MS 362, fos. 243–4.

43 *EP*, ii.437.

44 *EP*, ii.426.

45 *EP*, ii.425–6.

46 *EP*, ii.427–31; BL Stowe MS 362, fos. 259v–60v; USA Huntington Library, Ellesmere MS 488, 489.

Chapter 9

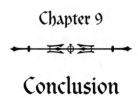

Conclusion

The focus of much of these chapters has been the ground covered by Neale and his recent critics, as well as the rejection of the earlier picture of constitutional turmoil driven by a minority of religiously fervent members. The older view which saw Parliament, and more particularly the Commons, as an intensely political body bent on self-advancement has given way to newer interpretations which emphasise that occasional conflicts should not hide the fact that the predominant function of Parliament – Lords, Commons, Crown – was to co-operate in making laws, some for major state purposes, and others for more localised, even personalised, purposes. It has been argued here that Parliament in Elizabeth's reign was often characterised by much greater opposition than Neale imagined. There was from time to time disenchantment with a Queen expected to live up to the demands of a political ideal she had herself helped to foster. Some of this arose from the fact that Lords and Commons were part of the same sections of society which provided governors at various levels, and which therefore shared many of the same assumptions and prejudices. There was a cohesiveness inherent in the very structure, business, and *raison d'être* of Parliament which at times spelt danger for Elizabeth.

Neale appreciated Elizabeth's isolation.

In our parliamentary history the person of the Queen is seen isolated in a unique and most significant way. On the succession question in 1566 she stood alone, against her Council (including Cecil) and her Parliament (including the Lords). In 1572 she withstood even more impassioned and concerted pressure and saved the life of Mary Queen of Scots: as Cecil bitterly remarked, the fault was not in 'us that are accounted inward councillors', but in 'the highest.'

Neale's interpretation of the isolation on these issues and others was, however, essentially a glorious one. A fair-minded Queen was able singlehandedly to withstand the pressures from her Protestant (Puritan?) subjects and to preserve an essentially 'English way' of life, broad rather than narrow and shunning 'what we today term the ideological State'.[1]

The Cecils, both William and Robert, and others would not have accepted such a picture. The role they played throughout the reign was a difficult one. At heart they were full-time ministers to the Queen who might also serve in the parliaments which occasionally assembled during the reign. Sometimes their fellow members appear to have expected them to behave as though they were primarily members of Parliament who should use their positions to influence the sovereign on behalf of the Houses. In fact, there can be little doubt now that they wished to use the temporary parliamentary base as a means of shaping Elizabeth's mind and determination so that she demonstrated an *obvious* solidarity with their own. Rarely, if ever, was this accomplished, and they and the other members had to be content with the Queen's sometimes obscure rhetoric which *said* that her care for them and the Church was assured. The tension inherent in Councillors' difficult position was also a persistent feature of the reign, perhaps nowhere demonstrated more graphically than in the monopolies issue in 1601.

There are other, related, problems with Neale's parliamentary picture, as yet not so readily appreciated by his critics. Parliament was necessarily much occupied from time to time with the great problem of the age, namely the survival of Protestantism and England in a largely Catholic Europe. In the first place, locating the 'opposition' in the so-called Puritan 'choir' naturally imposed a view of the pattern of the difficulties the Queen faced, for the intensity of those problems was seen to be connected with the fate of the religious agitation in the country, with the changing fortunes of 'Puritanism' as Neale saw it. Thus after the Queen had seen off the Presbyterian pushes of the 1580s, the remaining sessions of the reign seemed to be tame affairs in comparison, and if they occasionally amounted to something more substantial, as in the case of monopolies, then the Queen's superb political skills and judgement were still able to deal with them. The ideological warfare inherent in the 'precocious' organisation of the fringes of Protestantism was ephemeral, and 'not the least interesting feature of our story is the change in temper and character of the last parliaments of her reign'. As far as 1601 was concerned there was a marked tendency for him to believe that the phenomenon of a troublesome parliamentary session was a historical mirage. For Neale it is the *record* of 1601 (Townshend's journal) 'which distorts our vision of the *actuality*, and that can only become clear when the earlier sessions come into focus and the threat they posed to the prerogative snaps into sharp focus'.[2]

Neale retained throughout a clear belief in Elizabeth's natural political skill which saw her through troubled waters and left the dignity and mystery of monarchy largely untouched. There is no real place in his account for the view that Elizabeth had been a disappointing, if not an irresponsible, prince to her subjects, and that the best part of the political establishment had been repeatedly rebuffed and chronically frustrated by a leader whose judgement on some occasions appeared beyond belief. Elizabeth's determination to remain single exposed the regime to a degree of frailty in the present, and by highlighting its finiteness, promised a future which was dangerous, because uncertain. If all the other Tudors had spent considerable time on trying conspicuously to determine the future of their regimes, it was strange that Elizabeth seemed content not to do so. Indeed, when asked to take action it must have seemed that her refusal became more spirited and determined. This very basic issue increased the disappointment of her subjects and, as it remained unsolved, their responses evolved and developed an alarming degree of desperation.

These men in Parliament could not, however, be disloyal in the face of threats from Catholic Europe. Prevarication and empty promises from the Protestant English Queen would have to be suffered, though they clearly stuck in the gullet. It cannot have been good for the political health of the realm that the Queen was forced, time and time again, to rely solely on the mere fact of her existence as her primary, if not sole political weapon against her own governors and councillors, nobles and bishops. There had already been signs, as we have seen, that by the early 1570s the governing gentlemen of England doubted their sovereign's political judgement, and that this was a threat to the security of the realm, and therefore to their life and property. The repeated petitioning about safety and succession was

167

nothing if not a collective plea from the highest quarters of the land for the Queen to see sense, and men like Wentworth and Throckmorton are not so much extremists as men with fellow feelings which boiled over because they were unable to contain their incredulity. There is no doubt that the members who spoke in 1601 of the benefits of Elizabeth's long reign were being truthful and were fully aware of what they were saying: since James's birth in 1566 many of their kind had hardly been willing to face the Stuart succession. Her survival was a matter of national emotional and political investment. Holding her own against a combination of Catholic hostile forces highlighted the picture, and it was this which confirmed in a poignant way her mere Englishness. For many, however, Elizabeth's relative inactivity beyond merely existing and surviving was not enough. So what we have seen throughout is a gulf, albeit contained, between the elements of government which may have bordered on positive disenchantment. We cannot believe that they would have given the Queen full marks for her performance since her accession.

We might confirm this by imagining briefly how the parliamentary scene looked to the Queen herself. Historians have rightly emphasised the co-operative aspects of Parliament's work. Undeniably, the governing classes of England represented in Lords and Commons worked together for obvious reasons in obvious areas. The working relationship between Lords and Commons is itself a commentary on this theme, and it draws its force and vigour from the underlying fact that both Houses had an equal part in the process of reviewing the laws of the land. This naturally explains how disagreements and difficulties over important principles could sometimes arise. We should also expect to see, from both Houses, a spirited defence of positions which had been adopted, because this was how their role in reviewing the law sometimes became a reality.

It is, however, more difficult to see how the other main element in the picture, namely the Queen herself, always fitted in to this picture of co-operation. We see her chastising members and arguing that young hotheads had taken over the Commons, and it is hard to believe that she was comfortable in the parliamentary setting. Many wanted further reform of the Church, and Elizabeth had in fact been confronted not only with widely rather than narrowly supported wishes to consolidate the Protestant settlement, but her own men of goverment in state, and – for a time – the Church were among those actively pursuing such ambitions. Opposition in Parliament was more, not less, serious simply because it showed more cohesion among the governors of England, though much less among the Queen and her 'government' than we used to imagine. The religious and political differences revealed between the Queen and her leading subjects, in and out of the court and council circles, may be seen as differences among friends. They were of minor importance compared with the agreement over the need to defeat Catholicism. The fact remains, however, that Elizabeth demonstrated a keen sense of irritation when religion, for instance, was raised despite her instructions to the contrary.

She had wanted to use Parliament for her own purposes, and had been able to do that reasonably well. Parliament had confirmed her authority in the Church, as it had done for her father, but she expended much energy subsequently in defending it against Parliament itself, and not just a small coterie of 'Puritans' as Neale imagined. Parliament had turned out to be a parade ground on which commoners and members of the Lords, including the bishops themselves, could marshal a public challenge to her conduct of the supreme governorship. Her stubborn refusal to do much about it demonstrated the strength of the parliamentary settlement of 1559. The absence of positive reforming initiatives on her part meant that she remained supreme, though hardly superb in the eyes of ministers, secular and clerical. She had also been able to come to the Lords and Commons and ask for subsidies, which were granted without too much trouble and without too much bargaining. Even here, though, the gentlemen of England were careful about how they parted with their money, though they were also careful to maintain the notion that Queen and subject were at one in the defence of Protestant England and its peace and justice.

The idea of Protestant Elizabethan England – and its special, even unique, quality – was central to the parliamentary context for lawmaking and governing, and provided, if it was needed, a constant reminder of what Parliament was about. It may be suggested that this was indeed the common starting-point for the disagreements between Queen and subject, rather than any concept of 'choirs' or faction groups. This is not to deny that rival groups could sometimes exert a dynamic of their own. For example, there do appear to have been supporters of Whitfgift at work in the Commons, willing to oppose measures there which were unpalatable to him, though they could clearly be objectionable to others in their own right. Such manifestations of factional division, if that is what this was, do not hide the widespread disagreement with the Queen over important issues. The demolition of the notion of an *organised* opposition, such as the 'Puritan choir', makes way for something which more significant, because more broadly based. When Elizabeth felt affronted, and even justified herself *constitutionally* against pressure from Parliament, the political allies she thought she could rely on were either nowhere in sight, or were clearly lined up on the other side of the fence.[3]

Investigation of the matter of legislative initiative suggests that a high proportion of parliamentary bills were not inspired by those traditionally thought of as constituting the 'government'. In important areas, especially trade and even social policy, we need to be more prepared to see legislative activity as 'governor-inspired'. The work of Parliament was demonstrably based on the active participation of a broad group of men, and did not derive merely from those working in central government. Parliament was made up of men who by breeding and experience at local level, at least, saw themselves as natural governors. Francis Bacon said in 1601 that every man was 'bound to help the commonwealth the best he may'; and Hayward Townshend, referring to Bacon's words, added, 'much more is every man in his particular bound, being a member of this House, if he know any dangerous enormity towards the comonwealth that he would not only open it but, if it may be, repress it'. When Sir Francis Hastings went on to say that 'the Church and commonwealth are two twins which laugh and live together', he had taken only one small intellectual step from that position, but we have seen that its political implications were too explosive for the Queen to accept.[4]

All this matters because one of the criticisms of the older view of Parliament's work was that it was unduly preoccupied with controversial matters of high politics. As a result, not enough attention was paid to the work of making law which provided the bulk of the business of any session. More recently, this approach has developed into the beginnings of an appreciation that the *background* to making law is of interest in itself. We need to investigate why individuals and groups set out to secure the passage of new laws, and whose support was enlisted in the process. As detailed work on specific bills and acts proceeds, it will become evident how individual members of both Lords and Commons were involved in furthering the efforts of local interest groups in their legislative endeavours. This was simply because they could both be involved with particular causes by virtue of local connection through residence or some other relationship. It was always clear that when boroughs, for instance, pressed local aristocrats to be their patrons, and possibly gave them a share in nominating their parliamentary representatives, they might expect something in return. The possible importance of this in the business of parliamentary sessions cannot be underestimated, because it looks as though up to one in three of the bills introduced in some sessions may have been locally inspired. Certainly, in the second half of the reign, about 20 per cent of 'local' bills and acts were introduced into the Upper House, many of them affecting the lands of the local bishops or peers.[5]

In these cases, the object was to gain statutory endorsement for a particular cause, and therefore strengthen it in a unique way. At the parliamentary end of the process, lobbying support could become an extensive and expensive operation. The London Clothworkers appear to have been the most persistent group. While the subject of lobbying tactics needs further investigation, it is already clea that many devices were deployed by companies and groups who wished to further their own interests directly, or to prevent others stealing a march on them.[6] Wining and dining, 'sweeteners', soliciting information about the membership of relevant Commons' committees, and paying members for speaking in the interest of a particular group were all part of the wider parliamentary scene.[7] Legislation was desirable, for instance, because it could provide statutory protection for schools and hospitals, or the legal power for authorities to raise revenue locally to finance road or bridge repairs. It follows from this, however, that local ambitions of all sorts could clash with each other, and in such cases it seems that individual members of the Lords or Commons might be divided by the loyalty they showed to differing towns. Thus a dispute over the landing of goods on the river Severn saw not only Gloucester and Bristol on opposing sides, but also Burghley and Leicester, their respective supporters.[8] The latter also appears to have contributed, as Lord High Steward of Yarmouth, to the passing of an act in 1581 to restrict herring imports, contrary to the wishes of the powerful London Fishmongers.[9]

Elizabeth's parliaments

It is easy to appreciate how concern for the commonwealth which men like Hastings and Townshend voiced could encompass working for particular pieces of legislation promoted by small, often powerful groups. In the future, historians may turn their attentions to a more systematic exploration of the various approaches members brought to bear in their work, and of reviewing and making law. We have emphasised the importance of members' attitudes to the criteria employed in the formulation of law. These are aspects of an intellectual framework which, by any reckoning, must be crucial to an understanding of Parliamentary mentality. Some time ago a pioneer study of social attitudes among members in the later part of the reign indicated how the evidence may be used to probe the governing mind, and more recently studies of legislation on usury shed further light on the subject.[10] The increasing concern with interest groups itself will be an important part of the exploration. What may emerge is not so much a picture of the parliamentary procedures involved, but the philosophies and prejudices which produced laws in one form or another. Together with the problem of determining where the inititative for legislation really lay, there is a great deal of work to be done, and some of the answers may be unattainable. We now more fully appreciate that, in their entirety, the bills presented to Parliament's consideration arose from a variety of sources and initiatives, some officially inspired, some officially supported, some perhaps carrying the support of one or several Privy Councillors, some merely individually or locally originated, often by towns or other interest groups, and that it may not be possible to delineate *precisely* where ideas came from.[11] But when we recognise this, what we are witnessing is the essence of Parliament's nature, namely a gathering together of the sinews of English goverment in the broader sense.

NOTES

1 *EP*, i.419.

2 *EP*, ii.436–7.

3 See also Arthur Hall's case: Graves, 'Managing Elizabethan parliaments', p. 45, and pp. 43–6 for the Privy Councillors in Parliament.

4 BL Stowe MS 362, fos. 81v–2, 89, 253v–4.

5 Dean, 'Parliament and locality', pp. 146–8, 158, 161–2.

6 Archer, 'The London lobbies', esp. pp. 22, 34 and n. 130.

7 Dean, 'Public or private?', esp. pp. 532–5; see also Dean, 'London lobbies and Parliament'.

8 Dean, 'Parliament and locality', pp. 151–2.

9 Dean, 'Parliament and locality', p. 157 and Elton, 'Piscatorial politics'.

10 Kent, 'Attitudes of members of the House of Commons'; Jones, 'Religion in Parliament', pp. 118, 132–4.

11 Dean, 'Parliament and locality', pp. 139–62.

Appendix

PARLIAMENTARY SESSIONS OF ELIZABETH'S REIGN
(AND PRINCIPAL MATTERS REFERRED TO IN THE TEXT)

1   *1559: 23 January – 8 May*
Religious settlement – uniformity and supremacy. Queen's title confirmed. First fruits and tenths restored to Crown subsidy. Queen's marriage.

2   *1563: 11 January – 10 April*
Assurance of Queen's power. Succession. Artificers. Relief of poor. Artificers. Purveyors. Subsidy.

3   *1566–67: 30 September 1563 – 2 January 1567*
Succession. Alphabetical bills, including Bill A (Articles of religion). Subsidy.

4   *1571: 2 April – 29 May*
Treasons. Papal bulls. Northern rebels. Archbishop and licences. Alphabetical bills, especially Bills A and B. Coming to church. Prayer Book and Strickland. Subsidy.

5   *1572: 8 May – 30 June*
Queen's safety. Rites and ceremonies.

6   *1576: 8 February – 15 March*
Petitions on Church. Coming to church. Apparel. Forests. Stourton. Peter Wentworth. Subsidy.

7   *1581: 16 January – 18 March*
Obedience of subjects. Seditious words. Petitions on Church. Coming to church. Subsidy.

8   *1584–85: 23 November 1584 – 29 March 1585*
Petitions on Church. Turner's Bill and Book. Queen's safety (and Bond of Association). Jesuits. 1571 Act on Ministers. Sabbath. Fraudulent conveyances. Wardships. Subsidy.

9   *1586–87: 29 October 1586 – 23 March 1587*
Mary Queen of Scots. Sovereignty of Netherlands. Purveyors. Peter Wentworth. Cope's Bill and Book.

10   *1589: 4 February – 29 March*
Exchequer. Pluralities. Purveyance. Subsidy.

174

11   *1593: 19 February – 10 April*
Disloyal subjects/sectaries. Popish recusants (Five-Mile Act). Morice's bills

12   *1597–98: 24 October 1597 – 9 February 1598*
Tillage. Husbandry. Monopolies. Ecclesiastical fees. Marriage licences. Probate of wills.

13   *1601: 27 October – 19 December*
Monopolies. Pluralities. Sabbath. Exchequer. Ordnance .Subsidy.

Bibliography

MANUSCRIPTS

Hatfield House

London
British Library   Additional MSS. Cotton MSS. Harley MSS. Lansdowne
    MSS. Sloane MSS. Stowe MSS.
Historical Manuscripts Commission   Salisbury MSS.
Lambeth Palace
Public Record Office   State Papers.

Longleat
    Bath, Thynne MSS.

New York
    New York Library   Pierpont Morgan MSS.

Northampton
    Northamptonshire CRO   Finch Hatton MSS. Fitzwilliam of Milton
    MSS.

Oxford
    Bodleian Library   Rawlinson MSS.

San Marino, California
    Henry E. Huntington Library   Ellesmere Papers.

PRINTED SOURCES

S. Adams, 'The Dudley clientage and the House of Commons, 1559–1601',
    Parliamentary History, 8 (1989), 216–39.

J.D. Alsop, 'The theory and practice of Tudor taxation', *English Historical
    Review*, 97 (1982), 1–30.

J.D. Alsop, 'Parliament and taxation', in Dean and Jones (eds.) (1990), pp.
    91–116.

J.D. Alsop, 'Reinterpreting the Elizabethan Commons: the Parliamentary
    Session of 1566', *Journal of British Studies*, 29 (1990), 216–40.

I. Archer, 'The London lobbies in the later sixteenth century', *Historical
    Journal*, 31 (1988), 17–44.

176

Bibliography

G. Bowler, '"An axe or an acte": the Parliament of 1572 and resistance theory in early Elizabethan England', *Canadian Journal of History*, 19 (1984), 349–59.

C.W. Brooks, *Pettyfoggers and Vipers of the Commonwealth: the* 'Lower Branch' of the Legal Profession in Early Modern *England* (Cambridge, 1986).

J. Bruce (ed.), *Correspondence of Matthew Parker, D.D., Archbishop of Canterbury* (Parker's Society, Cambridge, 1853).

W.D.J. Cargill Thompson, *Studies in the Reformation: Luther to Hooker* (London, 1980).

P. Collinson, *The Elizabethan Puritan Movement* (London, 1965).

P. Collinson, 'Sir Nicholas Bacon and the Elizabethan *via media*', *Historical Journal*, 23 (1980), 255–73.

P. Collinson, *The Religion of Protestants: The Church in English Society, 1559–1625* (Oxford, 1982).

P. Collinson, 'The monarchical republic of Queen Elizabeth I', *Bulletin of the John Rylands Library*, 69 (1987), 394– 424.

P. Collinson, 'Puritans, men of business and Elizabethan parliaments', *Parliamentary History*, 7 (1988), 187–211.

P. Croft, 'Parliament, purveyance and the city of London, 1589–1608', *Parliamentary History*, 5 (1985), 9–34.

C. Cross, *The Royal Supremacy in the Elizabethan Church* (London, 1969).

J.R. Dasent *et al.* (eds.), *Acts of the Privy Council of England* (n.s., 46 vols., London, 1890–1964).

D.M. Dean, 'Parliament and locality', in Dean and Jones (eds.) (1990), pp. 139–62.

D.M. Dean, 'Enacting clauses and legislative initiative, 1584– 1601', *Bulletin of the Institute for Historical Research*, 57, no. 136 (1984), 140–8.

D.M. Dean, 'Public or private? London, leather and legislation in Elizabethan England', *Historical Journal*, 31 (1988), 525–48.

D.M. Dean, 'London lobbies and parliament: the case of the brewers and coopers in the Parliament of 1593', *Parliamentary History*, 8 (1989), 341–65.

D.M. Dean and N.L. Jones (eds.), *The Parliaments of Elizabethan England* (Oxford, 1990).

D.M. Dean and N.L. Jones, 'Introduction', in Dean and Jones (eds.) (1990), pp. 1–13.

S. D'Ewes, Sir, *The Journals of all the Parliaments during the Reign of Queen Elizabeth* (London, 1682).

Bibliography

A.G. Dickens, *The English Reformation* (2nd edition, London, 1989).

G.R. Elton, *Reform and Renewal: Thomas Cromwell and the Commonweal* (Cambridge, 1973).

G.R. Elton, *Studies in Tudor and Stuart Politics and Government* (3 vols., Cambridge, 1974–83).

G.R. Elton, *The Tudor Constitution: Documents and Commentary* (2nd edition, Cambridge, 1982).

G.R. Elton, *The Parliament of England* (Cambridge, 1986).

G.R. Elton, 'Piscatorial politics in the early parliaments of Elizabeth I', in *Business Life and Public Policy: Essays in Honour of D.C. Coleman*, ed. N. McKendrick and R.B. Outhwaite (Cambridge, 1986), pp. 1–20.

A.G. Fox and J.A. Guy, *Reassessing the Henrician Age: Humanism, Politics and Reform, 1500–1550* (Oxford, 1986).

F.S. Fussner (ed.), 'William Camden's "Discourse concerning the prerogative of the Crown"', *Proceedings of the American Philosophical Society*, 101 (1957), 204–15.

M.A.R. Graves, 'Thomas Norton the parliament man: an Elizabethan MP, 1559–81', *Historical Journal*, 23 (1980), 17–35.

M.A.R. Graves, *The House of Lords in the Parliaments of Edward VI and Mary: an Institutional Study* (Cambridge, 1981).

M.A.R. Graves, 'Managing Elizabethan parliaments', in Dean and Jones (eds.) (1990), pp. 37–64.

M.A.R. Graves, 'The management of the Elizabethan House of Commons: the Council's "men of business"', *Parliamentary History*, 2 (1983), 11–38.

M.A.R. Graves, *The Tudor Parliaments: Crown, Lords and Commons, 1485–1603* (London, 1985).

M.A.R. Graves, *Elizabethan Parliaments, 1559–1601* (London, 1987).

J.A. Guy, *Tudor England* (Oxford, 1988).

C. Haigh, *Elizabeth I* (London, 1988).

T.E. Hartley (ed.), *Proceedings in the Parliaments of Elizabeth I, i.1559–81* (Leicester, 1981).

T.E. Hartley, 'The sheriff and county elections', in Dean and Jones (eds.) (1990), pp. 163–89.

P.W. Hasler (ed.), *The House of Commons, 1558–1603* (3 vols., London, 1981).

W.P. Haugaard, *Elizabeth and the English Reformation: the Struggle for a Stable Settlement of Religion* (Cambridge, 1968).

F. Heal, 'Clerical tax collection under the Tudors', in *Continuity and Change*, ed. R. O'Day and F. Heal (Leicester, 1976), pp. 97–122.

D. Hirst, review of Kishlansky (1986) in *Albion*, 19 (1987), 428–34.

P.L. Hughes, *The Reformation in England* (3 vols., London, 1950–54).

P.L. Hughes and J.F. Larkin (eds.), *Tudor Royal Proclamations* (3 vols., New Haven, CT, 1964–69).

N.L. Jones, *Faith by Statute: Parliament and the Settlement of Religion* (London, 1982).

N.L. Jones, 'Religion in parliament', in Dean and Jones (eds.) (1990), pp. 117–38.

N.L. Jones and D.M. Dean (eds.), *Interest Groups and* Legislation in Elizabethan Parliaments: Essays presented to Sir Geoffrey Elton, special issue of *Parliamentary History*, 8 (1989).

J.R. Kent, 'Attitudes of members of the House of Commons to the regulation of personal conduct in late Elizabethan and early Stuart England', *Bulletin of the Institute of Historical Research*, 46 (1973), 41–71.

M. Kishlansky, *Parliamentary Selection: Social and Political Choice in Early Modern England* (Cambridge, 1986).

P. Lake, *Anglicans and Puritans? Presbyterianism and English Conformist Thought from Whitgift to Hooker* (London, 1988).

S.E. Lehmberg, *The Reformation Parliament 1529–36* (Cambridge, 1970).

S.E. Lehmberg, *The Later Parliaments of Henry VIII, 1536–47* (Cambridge, 1977).

M. Levine, *The Early Elizabethan Succession Question* (Stanford, CA, 1966).

J. Loach, review of Jones (1982) in *English Historical Review*, 101 (1986), 433–6.

A. Luders *et al.* (eds.), *Statutes of the Realm* (11 vols., London, 1810–28).

W.T. MacCaffrey, *The Shaping of the Elizabethan Regime: Elizabethan Politics, 1558–72* (London edition, 1969).

W.T. MacCaffrey, 'Parliament and foreign policy', in Dean and Jones (eds.) (1990), pp. 65–90.

D. MacCulloch, *Suffolk and the Tudors: Politics and Religion in an English County, 1500–1600* (Oxford, 1986).

R.B. Manning, *Village Revolts: Social Protest and Popular Disturbances in England, 1509–1640* (Oxford, 1988).

J.E. Neale, 'Peter Wentworth', *English Historical Review*, 39 (1924), 36–54, 175–205.

J.E. Neale, *The Elizabethan House of Commons* (London, 1949). J.E. Neale, *Elizabeth I and her Parliaments* (2 vols., London, 1953, 1957).

Bibliography

D.M. Palliser, *The Age of Elizabeth: England under the Later Tudors 1547–1603* (London, 1983).

C. Read, *Lord Burghley and Queen Elizabeth* (London, 1960). C. Russell, 'English parliaments 1593–1606: one epoch or two?', in Dean and Jones (eds.) (1990), pp. 191–213.

C. Russell, 'The nature of a parliament in early Stuart England', in *Before the English Civil War: Essays on Early Stuart Politics and Government*, ed. H. Tomlinson (London, 1983), pp. 123–50.

C. Russell, *The Causes of the English Civil War* (Oxford, 1990).

J.J. Scarisbrick, *Henry VIII* (London, 1968).

R. Schofield, 'Taxation and the political limits of the Tudor state', in *Law and Government under the Tudors*, ed. C. Cross, D. Loades and J.J. Scarisbrick (1988), pp. 227–55.

P. Slack, *Poverty in Tudor and Stuart England* (London, 1988).

J. Thirsk (ed.), *The Agrarian History of England and Wales iv. 1500–1640* (Cambridge, 1967).

J. Walter, 'A "rising of the people"? The Oxfordshire rising of 1596', *Past and Present*, 107 (1985), 90–143.

P. Williams, *The Tudor Regime* (Oxford, 1979).

Index

Index

Index